LEGAL TRAIL SERIES®

CONTRACTS

INCLUDING

ARTICLE 2 OF THE U.C.C.

[SALES & LEASES]

and selected provisions from

ARTICLE 5
&
ARTICLE 7

McLaren Legal Publishers

New York

ALSO AVAILABLE IN THIS SERIES:

Civil Procedure
Constitutional Law
Contracts
Corporations
Criminal Law
Criminal Procedure
Evidence
New York Civil Practice
Patent, Trademark & Copyright
Professional Responsibility
Property
Remedies
Secured Transactions
Torts

LEGAL TRAIL SERIES®

CONTRACTS

Second Edition

Peter R. Errico, Esq.

New York Law School

ISBN 10: 0-9820734-0-2
ISBN 13: 978-0-9820734-0-7

Published by
McLaren Legal Publishers LLC
552 Broadway, 3rd Floor
New York, NY 10012

www.mclarenpublishing.com
Email: contact@mclarenpublishing.com

Printed in the United States of America

HOW TO USE THIS BOOK

This law school study aid is a non-keyed, "generic" book. It may, depending on the topic reviewed, contain key, critical cases illustrative of the topic(s) reviewed. Generally, our Legal Trail Series® books reviewing rule-based courses will not contain caselaw, while our other non-rule based books will. Either way, all of our books are meant to provide an overall rigorous review of the course indicated and convey key concepts and points of law for general law school study. For a "keyed book" which tracks and analyses the cases of a specific casebook, please use our Legal Path Series® of keyed books.

"The U.C.C. Rules - Translated"

We have presented both the actual statutes from the U.C.C., relevant to the topic indicated, and our version of the same rule. That is, following each **ACTUAL** U.C.C Rule is our outlined version of the actual Rule, written in an easy-to-understand format and "translated" to exclude all of the codified "legalese" while retaining the critical essence of the Rule itself. For simple, straightforward clarity, our version of the rule is printed in the larger, **bolded** and ***italicized*** type, while the actual U.C.C. Rules presented in the smaller, non-bolded type.

"All of what you need, none of what you don't"

Our law school study guides give you exactly what you need to understand the key principles of the subject, including the sometimes elusive U.C.C. Rule. We are not a replacement for an in depth legal analysis of the subject matter covered; however, we do present what is absolutely critical in a very concise format.

Abbreviations used in this book

LOC	Buyer in the Ordinary Course
BOL	Bill of Lading
CIF	Cost, Insurance, Freight
C&F	Cost & Freight
DOT	Document of Title
GFP	Good Faith Purchaser
HDIC	Holder in Due Course
HDN	Holder by Due Negotiation
FAS	Freight along Side
FOB	Freight on Board
L/C	Letter of Credit
PMSI	Purchase Money Security Interest
S/I	Security Interest

* Use of the word "his" in this book is gender neutral and encompasses both "his" and "her."

TABLE OF CONTENTS

LEGAL TRAIL SERIES

UNIFORM COMMERCIAL CODE

ARTICLE 2 - SALES

PART 1

Short Title, General Construction and Subject Matter

§ 2-101. Short title.

This Article shall be known and may be cited as Uniform Commercial Code -- Sales. (5A Del. C. 1953, § 2-101; 55 Del. Laws, c. 349.)

RULE §2-101. Short title.

This Article shall be known and may be cited as Uniform Commercial Code

§ 2-102. Scope; certain security and other transactions excluded from this article.

Unless the context otherwise requires, this Article applies to transactions in goods; it does not apply to any transaction which although in the form of an unconditional contract to sell or present sale is intended to operate only as a security transaction nor does this Article impair or repeal any statute regulating sales to consumers, farmers or other specified classes of buyers. (5A Del. C. 1953, § 2-102; 55 Del. Laws, c. 349.)

RULE §2-102. Scope; certain security and other transactions excluded from this article.

Unless the context otherwise requires, this Article applies to transactions in goods; it does not apply to any transaction which although in the form of an unconditional contract to sell or present sale is intended to operate only as a security transaction nor does this Article impair or repeal any statute regulating sales to consumers, farmers or other specified classes of buyers

§ 2-103. Definitions and index of definitions.

(1) In this Article unless the context otherwise requires:

(a) "Buyer" means a person who buys or contracts to buy goods.

(b) "Good faith" in the case of a merchant means honesty in fact and the observance of reasonable commercial standards of fair dealing in the trade.

(c) "Receipt" of goods means taking physical possession of them.

(d) "Seller" means a person who sells or contracts to sell goods.

(2) Other definitions applying to this Article or to specified Parts thereof, and the sections in which they appear are:

"Acceptance". Section 2-606.
"Banker's credit". Section 2-325.
"Between merchants". Section 2-104.
"Cancellation". Section 2-106(4).
"Commercial unit". Section 2-105.
"Confirmed credit". Section 2-325.
"Conforming to contract". Section 2-106.
"Contract for sale". Section 2-106.
"Cover". Section 2-712.
"Entrusting". Section 2-403.
"Financing agency". Section 2-104.
"Future goods". Section 2-105.
"Goods". Section 2-105.
"Identification". Section 2-501.
"Installment contract". Section 2-612.
"Letter of Credit". Section 2-325.
"Lot". Section 2-105.
"Merchant". Section 2-104.
"Overseas". Section 2-323.
"Person in position of seller". Section 2-707.
"Present sale". Section 2-106.
"Sale". Section 2-106.
"Sale on approval". Section 2-326.
"Sale or return". Section 2-326.
"Termination". Section 2-106.

(3) The following definitions in other Articles apply to this Article:

"Check". Section 3-104.
"Consignee". Section 7-102.
"Consignor". Section 7-102.
"Consumer goods". Section 9-102.
"Dishonor". Section 3-502.
"Draft". Section 3-104.

(4) In addition Article 1 contains general definitions and principles of construction and interpretation applicable throughout this Article. (5A Del. C. 1953, § 2-103; 55 Del. Laws, c. 349; 72 Del. Laws, c. 401, § 6.)

Definitions: see above.

§ 2-104. Definitions: "merchant"; "between merchants"; "financing agency."

(1) "Merchant" means a person who deals in goods of the kind or otherwise by his occupation holds himself out as having knowledge or skill peculiar to the practices or goods involved in the transaction or to whom such knowledge or skill may be attributed by his employment of an agent or broker or other intermediary who by his occupation holds himself out as having such knowledge or skill.

(2) "Financing agency" means a bank, finance company or other person who in the ordinary course of business makes advances against goods or documents of title or who by arrangement with either the seller or the buyer intervenes in ordinary course to make or collect payment due or claimed under the contract for sale, as by purchasing or paying the seller's draft or making advances against it or by merely taking it for collection whether or not documents of title accompany the draft. "Financing agency" includes also a bank or other person who similarly intervenes between persons who are in the position of seller and buyer in respect to the goods (Section 2-707).

(3) "Between merchants" means in any transaction with respect to which both parties are chargeable with the knowledge or skill of merchants. (5A Del. C. 1953, § 2-104; 55 Del. Laws, c. 349.)

RULE §2-104. Definitions: "merchant"; "between merchants"; "financing agency."

A "Merchant" is a:

a) person who
b) deals in goods of the kind <u>or</u>
c) otherwise by his occupation holds himself out as having knowledge or skill peculiar to the goods involved

§ 2-105. Definitions: transferability; "goods"; "future goods"; "lot"; "commercial unit."

(1) "Goods" means all things (including specially manufactured goods) which are movable at the time of identification to the contract for sale other than the money in which the price is to be paid, investment securities (Article 8) and things in action. "Goods" also includes the unborn young of animals and growing crops and other identified things attached to realty as described in the section on goods to be severed from realty (Section 2-107).

(2) Goods must be both existing and identified before any interest in them can pass. Goods which are not both existing and identified are "future" goods. A purported present sale of future goods or of any interest therein operates as a contract to sell.

(3) There may be a sale of a part interest in existing identified goods.

(4) An undivided share in an identified bulk of fungible goods is sufficiently identified to be sold although the quantity of the bulk is not determined. Any agreed proportion of such a bulk or any quantity thereof agreed upon by number, weight or other measure may to the extent of the seller's interest in the bulk be sold to the buyer who then becomes an owner in common.

(5) "Lot" means a parcel or a single article which is the subject matter of a separate sale or delivery, whether or not it is sufficient to perform the contract.

(6) "Commercial unit" means such a unit of goods as by commercial usage is a single whole for purposes of sale and division of which materially impairs its character or value on the market or in use. A commercial unit may be a single article (as a machine) or a set of articles (as a suite of furniture or an assortment of sizes) or a quantity (as a bale, gross,

or carload) or any other unit treated in use or in the relevant market as a single whole. (5A Del. C. 1953, § 2-105; 55 Del. Laws, c. 349.)

RULE §2-105. Definitions: transferability; "goods"; "future goods"; "lot"; "commercial unit."

"Goods" are all things which are movable at the time they are identified to a contract.

a) <u>The Following are "Goods"</u>:

1. ***Unborn young animals***
2. ***Growing crops***
3. ***Other identified things attached to realty (as described in 2-107: "Goods to be severed From Realty")***

b) <u>The Following are NOT "Goods"</u>:

1. ***Money in which the price of the contract is to be paid***
2. ***Investment Securities (see Article 8)***
3. ***Things in Action***

§ 2-106. Definitions: "contract"; "agreement"; "contract for sale"; "sale"; "present sale"; "conforming" to contract; "termination"; "cancellation."

(1) In this Article unless the context otherwise requires "contract" and "agreement" are limited to those relating to the present or future sale of goods. "Contract for sale" includes both a present sale of goods and a contract to sell goods at a future time. A "sale" consists in the passing of title from the seller to the buyer for a price (Section 2-401). A "present sale" means a sale which is accomplished by the making of the contract.

(2) Goods or conduct including any part of a performance are "conforming" or conform to the contract when they are in accordance with the obligations under the contract.

(3) "Termination" occurs when either party pursuant to a power created by agreement or law puts an end to the contract otherwise than for its breach. On "termination" all obligations which are still executory on both sides are discharged but any right based on prior breach or performance survives.

(4) "Cancellation" occurs when either party puts an end to the contract for breach by the other and its effect is the same as that of "termination" except that the cancelling party also retains any remedy for breach of the whole contract or any unperformed balance. (5A Del. C. 1953, § 2-106; 55 Del. Laws, c. 349.)

RULE §2-106(1) Contract for Sale:

a. Limitation to Present and Future Sales of Goods: In this Article (unless the context otherwise requires) the terms "contract" and "agreement" are limited to those relating to the present or future sale of goods.

b. "Contract for Sale" - includes both:
1. A Present Sale of goods; and
2. A contract to sell goods at a Future Time.

c. "Sale" - a sale consists of the passing of title from the Seller to the Buyer for a price (as per §2-401).

d. "Present Sale" - a sale which is accomplished by the making of the contact.

§ 2-107. Goods to be severed from realty; recording.

(1) A contract for the sale of minerals or the like (including oil and gas) or a structure or its materials to be removed from realty is a contract for the sale of goods within this Article if they are to be severed by the seller but until severance a purported present sale thereof which is not effective as a transfer of an interest in land is effective only as a contract to sell.

(2) A contract for the sale apart from the land of growing crops or other things attached to realty and capable of severance without material harm thereto but not described in subsection (1) or of timber to be cut is a contract for the sale of goods within this Article whether the subject matter is to be severed by the buyer or by the seller even though it forms part of the realty at the time of contracting, and the parties can by identification effect a present sale before severance.

(3) The provisions of this section are subject to any third party rights provided by the law relating to realty records, and the contract for sale may be executed and recorded as a document transferring an interest in land and shall then constitute notice to third parties

of the buyer's rights under the contract for sale. (5A Del. C. 1953, § 2-107; 55 Del. Laws, c. 349; 64 Del. Laws, c. 152, § 3.)

NOTICE: The Delaware Code appearing on this site was prepared by the Division of Research of Legislative Council of the General Assembly with the assistance of the Government Information Center, under the supervision of the Delaware Code Revisors and the editorial staff of LexisNexis and includes effective legislation through 74 Delaware Laws c. 263, as well as c. 265-272, 274, 277, 282-287, 294 and 297, effective as of June 22, 2004.

RULE §2-107(1): Goods Severed By Seller:

a. The following is considered a Contract for the Sale of Goods (and therefore governed by Article 2) so long as the material being sold is to be Severed (i.e., removed) from the Realty (on which they are sold) by the <u>Seller:</u>

1. A contract for the sale of Natural Resources (including minerals, oil and gas) to be removed from the Realty; or

2. A contract for the sale of a Structure (or its materials) to be removed from the realty

b. Until such "goods" are severed from the Realty a purported sale of such material is:

1. Effective as a Contract to Sell

2. Not effective as a Transfer of Interest

RULE §2-107(2): Goods Severed By Buyer or Seller:

a. The following will be considered a Contract for the Sale of Goods if the material is to be severed by the <u>Buyer</u> or the <u>Seller:</u>

1. A contract to sell <u>Growing Crops</u> (separate from the land)

2. A contract to sell <u>Timber</u> to be cut

3. Other things attached to realty and capable of severance without material harm to the property (but not described in 2-107(1))

b. Such contracts are deemed Contracts for the Sale of Goods even though the "goods" form part of the Realty at the time the contract was made (therefore, the parties can effect a present sale before severance (by identifying the actual goods sold under the contract)).

***SALES TRANSACTION:* The transaction involved must be a Sale.**

UNIFORM COMMERCIAL CODE

ARTICLE 2 - SALES

PART 2

Form, Formation and Readjustment of Contract

§ 2-201. Formal requirements; statute of frauds.

(1) Except as otherwise provided in this section a contract for the sale of goods for the price of $500 or more is not enforceable by way of action or defense unless there is some writing sufficient to indicate that a contract for sale has been made between the parties and signed by the party against whom enforcement is sought or by his authorized agent or broker. A writing is not insufficient because it omits or incorrectly states a term agreed upon but the contract is not enforceable under this paragraph beyond the quantity of goods shown in such writing.

(2) Between merchants if within a reasonable time a writing in confirmation of the contract and sufficient against the sender is received and the party receiving it has reason to know its contents, it satisfies the requirements of subsection (1) against such party unless written notice of objection to its contents is given within ten days after it is received.

(3) A contract which does not satisfy the requirements of subsection (1) but which is valid in other respects is enforceable.

(a) if the goods are to be specially manufactured for the buyer and are not suitable for sale to others in the ordinary course of the seller's business and the seller, before notice of repudiation is received and under circumstances which reasonably indicate that the goods are for the buyer, has made either a substantial beginning of their manufacture or commitments for their procurement; or

(b) if the party against whom enforcement is sought admits in his pleading, testimony or otherwise in court that a contract for sale was made, but the contract is not enforceable under this provision beyond the quantity of goods admitted; or

(c) with respect to goods for which payment has been made and accepted or which have been received and accepted (Section 2-606). (5A Del. C. 1953, § 2-201; 55 Del. Laws, c. 349.)

RULE §2-201: Formal Requirements of a Contract:

(1) Statute of Frauds:

- ***a. A Contract for the Sale of Goods for z $500 must be in writing to be enforceable by way of action or defense (except as otherwise provided in this section).***
- ***b. The Writing Requirement:***
  1. ***The writing need only indicate that a contract for sale has been made between the parties***
  2. ***The writing must be signed by the party against whom enforcement is sought (or his authorized agent or broker (ex: if Seller is suing Buyer, Buyer's signature must be on the writing)).***
  3. ***A writing is not insufficient if it omits or incorrectly states an agreed upon term.***
- ***c. The Contract will not be enforceable under §2-201(1) beyond the quantity of goods shown in such writing.***

(2) Contract Between Merchants:

- ***a. Merchant's Confirmation: A Merchant may satisfy the requirements of writing (§2-201(1)) by sending the other Merchant party a confirmation of the contract.***
- ***b. Notice of Objection: The confirmation will be an effective writing unless the party receiving the confirmation gives the sender a written notice of objection within 10 Days after it received the confirmation.***
- ***c. If the party receiving the confirmation does not properly object to it, it will be effective if:***
  1. ***The writing is in confirmation of the contract; and***
  2. ***It is also sufficient to hold the sender responsible; and***
  3. ***It is sent within a reasonable time after the contract was created; and***
  4. ***The party receiving the confirmation has reason to know its contents***

(3) A contract which does not satisfy the writing requirements in

§2-201(1) (but is valid in all other respects), will still be enforceable if:

(a) The Goods Are To Be Specially Manufactured:

1. ***The goods are to be specially manufactured for the Buyer; and***
2. ***The goods are not suitable for sale to others in the Ordinary Course of the Seller's Business; and***
3. ***The Seller has either substantially begun their manufacture or made commitments to obtain them:***
   - ***a. Before any notice of repudiation was received and b. Under circumstances which reasonably indicate that the goods are for the Buyer***

or (b) An Admission Is Made

1. ***If the party against whom enforcement is sought admits (in his pleadings, testimony, or otherwise in court) that a contract for sale was made, the writing requirement will be satisfied.***
2. ***The contract is only enforceable (under this provision) up to the quantity of goods admitted.***

or (c) The Goods Under The Contract Have Been Accepted

1. ***Payment has been made and accepted; or***
2. ***Goods have been received and accepted (as per §2-606)***

§ 2-202. Final written expression: parol or extrinsic evidence.

Terms with respect to which the confirmatory memoranda of the parties agree or which are otherwise set forth in a writing intended by the parties as a final expression of their agreement with respect to such terms as are included therein may not be contradicted by evidence of any prior agreement or of a contemporaneous oral agreement but may be explained or supplemented

(a) by course of dealing or usage of trade (Section 1-205) or by course of performance (Section 2-208); and

(b) by evidence of consistent additional terms unless the court finds the writing to have been intended also as a complete and exclusive statement of the terms of the agreement. (5A Del. C. 1953, § 2-202; 55 Del. Laws, c. 349.)

RULE §2-202: Final Written Expression; Parol or Extrinsic Evidence:

1. ***Final Written Expression:* The following are considered Final Written Expressions of the parties:**
   a. ***Agreed upon terms reflected in a Confirmatory Memorandum; or***
   b. ***Terms set forth in a Writing which were intended to be a Final Expression of their agreement (on those terms)***

2. ***Writing Cannot Be Contradicted: The terms of a Final Written Expression CANNOT be contradicted by evidence of any:***
   a. ***Prior Agreement; or***
   b. ***Contemporaneous Oral Agreement***

3. ***Writing May Be Explained: A Final Written Expression may, however, be explained or supplemented by:***
   (a) The Course of Dealing or Usage of Trade (§1-205) or by the Course of Performance (§2-208); and
   (b) Evidence of consistent additional terms, unless the court finds the writing was intended by both parties as a complete and exclusive statement of all the terms of the agreement

§ 2-203. Seals inoperative.

The affixing of a seal to a writing evidencing a contract for sale or an offer to buy or sell goods does not constitute the writing a sealed instrument and the law with respect to sealed instruments does not apply to such a contract or offer. (5A Del. C. 1953, § 2-203; 55 Del. Laws, c. 349.)

RULE §2-203. Seals inoperative.

The affixing of a seal to a writing evidencing a contract for sale or an offer to buy or sell goods does not constitute the writing a sealed instrument and the law with respect to sealed instruments does not apply to such a contract or offer.

§ 2-204. Formation in general.

(1) A contract for sale of goods may be made in any manner sufficient to show agreement, including conduct by both parties which recognizes the existence of such a contract.

(2) An agreement sufficient to constitute a contract for sale may be found even though the moment of its making is undetermined.

(3) Even though one or more terms are left open a contract for sale does not fail for indefiniteness if the parties have intended to make a contract and there is a reasonably certain basis for giving an appropriate remedy. (5A Del. C. 1953, § 2-204; 55 Del. Laws, c. 349.)

RULE §2-204: Formation of a Contract:

(1) Creation of Contract: A Contract for the Sale of Goods may be created by:
- ***a. The conduct of both parties (which recognizes the existence of such a contract); or***
- ***b. Any other manner sufficient to show agreement (written, oral or otherwise (subject to Statute of Frauds (§2-201))).***

(2) Time of Creation Not Certain: An agreement sufficient to constitute a contract for sale may be found even though the exact moment the contract was created is undetermined.

(3) Open Terms:

A contract will not fail for indefiniteness if one or more terms are left open, if:

- ***a. The parties have intended to make a contract; and***
- ***b. There is a reasonably certain basis for giving an appropriate remedy***

§ 2-205. Firm offers.

An offer by a merchant to buy or sell goods in a signed writing which by its terms gives assurance that it will be held open is not revocable, for lack of consideration, during the time stated or if no time is stated for a reasonable time, but in no event may such period of irrevocability exceed three months; but any such term of assurance on a form supplied by the offeree must be separately signed by the offeror. (5A Del. C. 1953, § 2-205; 55 Del. Laws, c. 349.)

RULE §2-205: Firm Offers:

1. "Firm Offer" - an offer which:

- ***a. Is made by a <u>Merchant</u>; and***
- ***b. Is evidenced by a <u>Signed</u> Writing; and***
- ***c. By its terms, gives assurance that the offer will be held open***

2. A Firm Offer is <u>not revocable</u> for lack of consideration.

3. Effectiveness of Firm Offer:

- ***a. The period of time in which a Firm Offer is irrevocable is either:***
  - ***1. For the time stated in the Firm Offer***
  - ***2. For a reasonable time, if no time is stated***
- ***b. The period of irrevocability may not exceed <u>3 Months</u>***

4. <u>Firm Offer on Offer's Form:</u> Any terms of assurance in a Firm Offer which is made on a form supplied by the <u>offeree</u> must be separately signed by the offeror.

§ 2-206. Offer and acceptance in formation of contract.

(1) Unless otherwise unambiguously indicated by the language or circumstances

(a) an offer to make a contract shall be construed as inviting acceptance in any manner and by any medium reasonable in the circumstances;

(b) an order or other offer to buy goods for prompt or current shipment shall be construed as inviting acceptance either by a prompt promise to ship or by the prompt or current shipment of conforming or non-conforming goods, but such a shipment of non-conforming goods does not constitute an acceptance if the seller seasonably notifies the buyer that the shipment is offered only as an accommodation to the buyer.

(2) Where the beginning of a requested performance is a reasonable mode of acceptance an offeror who is not notified of acceptance within a reasonable time may treat the offer as having lapsed before acceptance. (5A Del. C. 1953, § 2-206; 55 Del. Laws, c. 349.)

RULE §2-206: Offer and Acceptance in Formation of Contract:

(1) Unless otherwise <u>unambiguously</u> indicated by the language or circumstances:

(a) An Offer to Make a Contract:

1. ***An offer to make a contract is considered to be inviting acceptance.***
2. ***<u>Mode of Acceptance:</u> Acceptance to such an offer may be made in any manner and by any medium reasonable under the circumstances.***

(b) An Order or Other Offer to Buy Goods for Prompt Shipment:

1. ***An order or offer to buy goods for prompt or current shipment is considered to be inviting acceptance.***
2. ***<u>Mode of Acceptance:</u> Acceptance to such an offer may be made either by:***

a. A prompt promise to ship; or
b. Prompt or Current Shipment (of conforming or non-conforming goods)

3. <u>Shipment of Non-Conforming Goods:</u> The shipment of non-conforming goods does not constitute acceptance of the Buyer's offer if the Seller seasonably notifies the Buyer that the shipment was offered only as an "accommodation" to the Buyer.

(2) <u>Reasonable Time of Acceptance:</u> An offeror who is not notified of acceptance within a reasonable time may treat the offer as having lapsed before acceptance even if the beginning of the offer's performance was a reasonable mode of acceptance.

§ 2-207. Additional terms in acceptance or confirmation.

(1) A definite and seasonable expression of acceptance or a written confirmation which is sent within a reasonable time operates as an acceptance even though it states terms additional to or different from those offered or agreed upon, unless acceptance is expressly made conditional on assent to the additional or different terms.

(2) The additional terms are to be construed as proposals for addition to the contract. Between merchants such terms become part of the contract unless:

(a) the offer expressly limits acceptance to the terms of the offer;

(b) they materially alter it; or

(c) notification of objection to them has already been given or is given within a reasonable time after notice of them is received.

(3) Conduct by both parties which recognizes the existence of a contract is sufficient to establish a contract for sale although the writings of the parties do not otherwise establish a contract. In such case the terms of the particular contract consist of those terms on which the writings of the parties agree, together with any supplementary terms incorporated under this subtitle. (5A Del. C. 1953, § 2-207; 55 Del. Laws, c. 349.)

RULE §2-207: Additional Terms in Acceptance or Confirmation (Counteroffer):

(1) Acceptance With Different Terms:

a) The following operates as an acceptance even if it states <u>additional</u> or <u>different</u> terms from the offer if it is made as a:

1. Definite and seasonable expression of acceptance which is sent within a reasonable time; or

2. Written Confirmation which is sent within a reasonable time

b) If Acceptance is expressly made conditional to the offeror's acceptance of the offer's additional or different terms, then it is considered a counteroffer (and not an acceptance).

(2) Additional Terms:

i) <u>Between Non-Merchants:</u> Additional terms shall be construed as proposed additions to the contract.

ii) <u>Between Merchants:</u> Additional terms shall become part of the contract unless:

(a) The Offer expressly limits acceptance to the terms of the offer; or

(b) The additional terms materially alter the offer; or

(c) Notification of objection to the additional terms has already been given (or is given within a reasonable time after notice of the additional terms is received)

(3) Contracts Implied By Conduct:

a. <u>Conduct</u> by both parties which recognizes the existence of a contract is sufficient to establish a contract for sale (even though the writings of the parties do not otherwise establish one).

b. <u>Terms of Contracts Implied from Conduct:</u> The terms of such a contract (implied by the parties' conduct) shall be:

1. Those terms on which the writings of the parties

agree; and

2. Any supplementary terms incorporated under any other provision of this Act

§ 2-208. Course of performance or practical construction.

(1) Where the contract for sale involves repeated occasions for performance by either party with knowledge of the nature of the performance and opportunity for objection to it by the other, any course of performance accepted or acquiesced in without objection shall be relevant to determine the meaning of the agreement.

(2) The express terms of the agreement and any such course of performance, as well as any course of dealing and usage of trade, shall be construed whenever reasonable as consistent with each other; but when such construction is unreasonable, express terms shall control course of performance and course of performance shall control both course of dealing and usage of trade (Section 1-205).

(3) Subject to the provisions of the next section on modification and waiver, such course of performance shall be relevant to show a waiver or modification of any term inconsistent with such course of performance. (5A Del. C. 1953, § 2-208; 55 Del. Laws, c. 349.)

RULE §2-208: Construction of Contract:

(1) When Course of Performance Relevant: The <u>Course of Performance</u> (accepted or acquiesced in without objection) will be relevant in determining the meaning of the agreement between the parties when:

- ***a. The contract for sale involves repeated occasions for performance by either party; and***
- ***b. The non-performing party knows the nature of the other party's performance; and***
- ***c. The non-performing party had an opportunity to object to the nature of that performance***

(2) Interpretation of Contract:

- ***a) When interpreting the terms of a contract, the following factors shall be construed to be <u>consistent</u>***

with each other whenever reasonable:

1. The Express Terms of the agreement; and

2. Any Course of Performance; and

3. Any Course of Dealing; and

4. Any Usage of Trade

b) When it is unreasonable to read the above factors consistently, then:

1. The Express Terms - shall be used to construe the "Course of Performance;" and

2. The Course of Performance - shall be used to construe both

a) The "Course of Dealing;" and

b) The "Usage of Trade" (as per §1-205)

(3) The Course of Performance shall be relevant to show the existence of a waiver or modification of any term inconsistent with such Course of Performance (subject to §2-209).

§ 2-209. Modification, rescission and waiver.

(1) An agreement modifying a contract within this Article needs no consideration to be binding.

(2) A signed agreement which excludes modification or rescission except by a signed writing cannot be otherwise modified or rescinded, but except as between merchants such a requirement on a form supplied by the merchant must be separately signed by the other party.

(3) The requirements of the statute of frauds section of this Article (Section 2-201) must be satisfied if the contract as modified is within its provisions.

(4) Although an attempt at modification or rescission does not satisfy the requirements of subsection (2) or (3) it can operate as a waiver.

(5) A party who has made a waiver affecting an executory portion of the contract may retract the waiver by reasonable notification received by the other party that strict performance will be required of any term waived, unless the retraction would be unjust in

view of a material change of position in reliance on the waiver. (5A Del. C. 1953, § 2-209; 55 Del. Laws, c. 349.)

RULE §2-209: Modification, Rescission and Waiver:

(1) No Consideration Required for Modification: A modification of a sales contract does not require consideration to be binding.

(2) Writing Requirement:

a. An agreement cannot be rescinded or modified without a signed writing if the original agreement:

1) Is in <u>writing;</u> and

2) Is <u>signed;</u> and

3) Requires that modifications or rescissions be made with a signed writing

b. Such a term (requiring a modification or rescission to be in writing) must be <u>separately signed</u> if:

1) One party is not a Merchant; and

2) The term is on a form supplied by the party who is a Merchant

(3) Statute of Frauds Requirement: The requirements of the Statute of Frauds (§2-201) must be satisfied if the modified contract falls under §2-201(1) (i.e. it is or is modified to be a Contract for the Sale of Goods for >_ $500).

(4) Creation of Waiver: Although an attempt to modify or rescind a Contract fails (because it is not a signed writing (§2-209(2) or (3) above)), it can operate as a <u>Waiver.</u>

(5) Retraction of Waiver:

a. A party who has made a waiver affecting an executory portion of a contract may retract the waiver by giving reasonable notice to the other party that <u>Strict Performance will be required</u> of any term waived.

b. In order for the retraction of the waiver to be effective, the other party must receive the notification requiring strict performance.
c. A party will not be able to retract such a waiver if it would be unjust in view of a material change of position in reliance on the waiver.

§ 2-210. Delegation of performance; assignment of rights.

(1) A party may perform his duty through a delegate unless otherwise agreed or unless the other party has a substantial interest in having his original promisor perform or control the acts required by the contract. No delegation of performance relieves the party delegating of any duty to perform or any liability for breach.

(2) Except as otherwise provided in Section 9-406, unless otherwise agreed all rights of either seller or buyer can be assigned except where the assignment would materially change the duty of the other party, or increase materially the burden or risk imposed on him by his contract, or impair materially his chance of obtaining return performance. A right to damages for breach of the whole contract or a right arising out of the assignor's due performance of his entire obligation can be assigned despite agreement otherwise.

(3) The creation, attachment, perfection, or enforcement of a security interest in the seller's interest under a contract is not a transfer that materially changes the duty of or increases materially the burden or risk imposed on the buyer or impairs materially the buyer's chance of obtaining return performance within the purview of subsection (2) unless, and then only to the extent that, enforcement actually results in a delegation of material performance of the seller. Even in that event, the creation, attachment, perfection, and enforcement of the security interest remain effective, but (i) the seller is liable to the buyer for damages caused by the delegation to the extent that the damages could not reasonably be prevented by the buyer, and (ii) a court having jurisdiction may grant other appropriate relief, including cancellation of the contract for sale or an injunction against enforcement of the security interest or consummation of the enforcement.

(4) Unless the circumstances indicate the contrary a prohibition of assignment of "the contract" is to be construed as barring only the delegation to the assignee of the assignor's performance.

(5) An assignment of "the contract" or of "all my rights under the contract" or an assignment in similar general terms is an assignment of rights and unless the language or the circumstances (as in an assignment for security) indicate the contrary, it is a delegation of performance of the duties of the assignor and its acceptance by the assignee

constitutes a promise by him to perform those duties. This promise is enforceable by either the assignor or the other party to the original contract.

(6) The other party may treat any assignment which delegates performance as creating reasonable grounds for insecurity and may without prejudice to his rights against the assignor demand assurances from the assignee (Section 2-609). (5A Del. C. 1953, § 2-210; 55 Del. Laws, c. 349; 72 Del. Laws, c. 401, § 7.)

RULE §2-210: Delegation of Performance; Assignment of Rights:

(1) Delegation:

- ***a. A party may perform his duty through a <u>delegate</u> unless:***
  - ***1. The other party has a substantial interest in having his original promisor perform or control the acts required by the contract; or***
  - ***2. The parties otherwise agree***
- ***b. Delegation of performance <u>does not</u> relieve the delegating party of any <u>duty to perform</u> or <u>liability for breach.</u>***

(2) Assignment:

- ***a. All the rights of a Seller or Buyer may be assigned unless:***
  - ***1. The parties otherwise agree; or***
  - ***2. The assignment would either:***
    - ***a) Materially Change the Duty of the other party (ex: Seller is a N.Y. company. It promises to ship goods to Buyer in NJ; Buyer cannot assign his rights to Assignee without Seller's consent if Assignee is a Hong Kong company, since it would cost Seller substantially more to ship its goods to Hong Kong and to set up and enforce a payment system); or***
    - ***b) Materially Increase the Burden or Risk imposed on the other party; or***
    - ***c) Materially Impair the Chance of Return Performance***

to the other party (ex: Buyer assigns his obligation to Assignee, who has a poor credit history)

b. <u>Assignment Despite Agreement:</u> The following rights can be assigned even if the parties agreed otherwise:

1. A right to damages for breach of the whole contract

2. A right arising out of the Assignor's due performance of his entire obligation

(3) Prohibiting Assignment: A clause prohibiting the assignment of "the contract" is to be construed as barring only the delegation to the consignee of the assignor's <u>performance</u> (unless the circumstances indicate otherwise).

(4) Effect of Assignment:

a. The following terms denote an "Assignment of Rights" (unless the language or circumstances indicate otherwise):

1. An assignment of "the contract"

2. An assignment of "all my rights under the contract"

3. An assignment in similar general terms

b. <u>Terms of Assignment:</u>

1. Such an assignment is a delegation of performance of the assignor's duties to the assignee.

2. Acceptance by the assignee constitutes a promise by the assignee to perform those duties.

3. This promise is enforceable by either the assignor or the Other party (to the original contract).

(5) Demand for Assurance:

Upon delegation to the assignee, the non-assigning original party may, without prejudice:

a. Treat any assignment which delegates performance as creating a reasonable grounds for insecurity (as per §2-609); and

b. <u>Demand assurances from the assignee</u> (as per §2-609) that any delegated duties will be performed

UNIFORM COMMERCIAL CODE

ARTICLE 2 - SALES

PART 3

General Obligation and Construction of Contract

§ 2-301. General obligations of parties.

The obligation of the seller is to transfer and deliver and that of the buyer is to accept and pay in accordance with the contract. (5A Del. C. 1953, § 2-301; 55 Del. Laws, c. 349.)

RULE §2-301: General Obligations of Parties:

1. ***Obligation of the Seller: Transfer and Deliver the goods in accordance with the contract.***
2. ***Obligation of the Buyer: Accept and Pay for the goods in accordance with the contract.***

§ 2-302. Unconscionable contract or clause.

(1) If the court as a matter of law finds the contract or any clause of the contract to have been unconscionable at the time it was made the court may refuse to enforce the contract, or it may enforce the remainder of the contract without the unconscionable clause, or it may so limit the application of any unconscionable clause as to avoid any unconscionable result.

(2) When it is claimed or appears to the court that the contract or any clause thereof may be unconscionable the parties shall be afforded a reasonable opportunity to present evidence as to its commercial setting, purpose and effect to aid the court in making the determination. (5A Del. C. 1953, § 2-302; 55 Del. Laws, c. 349.)

RULE §2-302: Unconscionable Contract or Clause:

(1) Treatment of Unconscionable Contracts or Clauses: If the court finds (as a matter of law) a contract or any clause of the contract to have been unconscionable at the time it was made, the court may:

- ***a. Refuse to enforce the entire contract; or***
- ***b. Refuse to enforce only the unconscionable portions of the contract; or***
- ***c. Limit the application of any unconscionable clause to avoid any unconscionable result***

(2) Proving Unconscionability:

- ***a. When a contract clause appears unconscionable, or when a party claims it is unconscionable, the parties shall have a reasonable opportunity to present evidence (to aid the court in making its determination).***
- ***b. Evidence presented to the court may include evidence as to:***
  - ***1. The <u>commercial setting</u> of the contract; and***
  - ***2. The <u>purpose</u> of the contract; and***
  - ***3. The <u>intended effect</u> of the contract***

§ 2-303. Allocation or division of risks.

Where this Article allocates a risk or a burden as between the parties "unless otherwise agreed", the agreement may not only shift the allocation but may also divide the risk or burden. (5A Del. C. 1953, § 2-303; 55 Del. Laws, c. 349.)

Where this Article allocates a risk or a burden as between the parties "unless otherwise agreed", the agreement may not only shift the allocation but may also divide the risk or burden.

§ 2-304. Price payable in money, goods, realty, or otherwise.

(1) The price can be made payable in money or otherwise. If it is payable in whole or in part in goods each party is a seller of the goods which he is to transfer.

(2) Even though all or part of the price is payable in an interest in realty the transfer of the goods and the seller's obligations with reference to them are subject to this Article, but not the transfer of the interest in realty or the transferor's obligations in connection therewith. (5A Del. C. 1953, § 2-304; 55 Del. Laws, c. 349.)

RULE §2-304: Price Payable:

(1) Payment with Money or Goods:

- ***a. The price of a contract may be payable in Money or otherwise.***
- ***b. If the contract is payable in goods (in whole or in pan), each party is considered a Seller of the goods which he is to transfer.***

(2) Payment with Realty:

- ***a. All contracts may be paid with interests in realty.***
- ***b. Applicable Laws Governing Contracts for the Sale of Goods Which Are Paid with Realty:***
    - ***1. Article 2 governs:***
        - ***a) The Seller's obligations with reference to the goods; and***
        - ***b) Laws relating to the Transfer of the goods***
    - ***2. Article 2 will not govern:***
        - ***a) Laws relating to the Transfer of Interest in the Realty; and***

b) The transferor's obligations in connection with the Transfer of the Realty

§ 2-305. Open price term.

(1) The parties if they so intend can conclude a contract for sale even though the price is not settled. In such a case the price is a reasonable price at the time for delivery if

(a) nothing is said as to price; or

(b) the price is left to be agreed by the parties and they fail to agree; or

(c) the price to be fixed in terms of some agreed market or other standard as set or recorded by a third person or agency and it is not so set or recorded.

(2) A price to be fixed by the seller or by the buyer means a price for him to fix in good faith.

(3) When a price left to be fixed otherwise than by agreement of the parties fails to be fixed through fault of one party the other may at his option treat the contract as cancelled or himself fix a reasonable price.

(4) Where, however, the parties intend not to be bound unless the price be fixed or agreed and it is not fixed or agreed there is no contract. In such a case the buyer must return any goods already received or if unable so to do must pay their reasonable value at the time of delivery and the seller must return any portion of the price paid on account. (5A Del. C. 1953, § 2-305; 55 Del. Laws, c. 349.)

RULE §2-305: Open Price Term

(1) Price Unsettled:

i) If the parties intend, they can conclude a contract for sale even if they have not yet settled on a price (subject to §2-305(4) below).

ii) The price of the contract shall be a reasonable price <u>at the time</u> <u>for delivery</u> if:

(a) Nothing is said about the price; or

(b) The price is left to be agreed upon by the parties,

and they fail to agree; or

(c) The price is to be fixed in terms of some agreed market which has not been set or recorded (or other standard as set or recorded by a third person or agency (ex: setting the price of cotton at $5.00 over the COMEX price on the date of delivery)) (see §2-305(3) below for the effects of not fixing price).

(2) A "price to be fixed by the Seller/Buyer" - means a price fixed by him in <u>Good Faith.</u>

(3) Fault of a Party:

If the price of a contract is left to be fixed (other than by agreement of the parties), and that price fails to be fixed due to the fault of one party, the other party may:

1. Treat the contract as canceled; or

2. Fix a reasonable price on his own

(4) Failure of Contract:

a) There will be <u>no contract</u> if the parties intend not to be bound unless the price is fixed or agreed upon, and it is not.

b) <u>Consequences If Contract Fails Due to Absence of Price:</u>

1. Buyer's Obligations - the Buyer must:

a. Return any goods already received; or

b. If the Buyer is unable to return the goods she must Pay the Seller the reasonable value of the goods at <u>the time of delivery,</u>

2. Seller's Obligations - The Seller must return any portion of the price paid on account.

§ 2-306. Output, requirements and exclusive dealings.

(1) A term which measures the quantity by the output of the seller or the requirements of the buyer means such actual output or requirements as may occur in good faith, except that no quantity unreasonably disproportionate to any stated estimate or in the absence of

a stated estimate to any normal or otherwise comparable prior output or requirements may be tendered or demanded.

(2) A lawful agreement by either the seller or the buyer for exclusive dealing in the kind of goods concerned imposes unless otherwise agreed an obligation by the seller to use best efforts to supply the goods and by the buyer to use best efforts to promote their sale. (5A Del. C. 1953, § 2-306; 55 Del. Laws, c. 349.)

RULE §2-306: Output, Requirements, and Exclusive Dealings Contracts

(1) Output & Requirement Contracts:

a. Terms Measuring Quantity:

1. "Output Term" - a term which measures the quantity of the contract by the Seller's output (i.e. "Total Production" contract).

2. "Requirement Term" - a term which measures the quantity of the contract by the requirements of the Buyer (i.e. "Total Needs" contract).

b. Good Faith Requirement:

1. "Output" and "Requirement" terms refer to actual output and requirements that occur in Good Faith.

2. Estimates - if an estimate of output or requirement is included in the agreement, no quantity unreasonably disproportionate to the estimate may be:

a) Tendered by the Seller; or

b) Demanded by the Buyer

3. In absence of a stated estimate, no quantity which is more than any normal or comparable prior output or requirement may be:

a) Tendered by the Seller; or

b) Demanded by the Buyer

(2) Exclusive Dealings - "Best Efforts Test": A lawful agreement by either a Seller or Buyer for Exclusive Dealing (in the kind

of goods concerned) creates the following obligations (unless otherwise agreed):

a) Exclusive Right to Sell: Obligation by the Seller to use its Best Efforts to supply the goods

b) Exclusive Right to Buy: Obligation by Buyer to use its Best Efforts to promote the sale of such goods

§ 2-307. Delivery in single lot or several lots.

Unless otherwise agreed all goods called for by a contract for sale must be tendered in a single delivery and payment is due only on such tender but where the circumstances give either party the right to make or demand delivery in lots the price if it can be apportioned may be demanded for each lot. (5A Del. C. 1953, § 2-307; 55 Del. Laws, c. 349.)

RULE §2-307: Delivery in Single Lot or Several Lots:

1) Single Delivery: Unless otherwise agreed:
  a. All goods called for by a contract for sale must be Tendered in a single delivery; and
  b. Payment is due only upon such tender.

2) If the circumstances allow either party to make or demand delivery in separate lots, then the price can be apportioned and demanded for each delivery.

§ 2-308. Absence of specified place for delivery.

Unless otherwise agreed

(a) the place for delivery of goods is the seller's place of business or if he has none his residence; but

(b) in a contract for sale of identified goods which to the knowledge of the parties at the time of contracting are in some other place, that place is the place for their delivery; and

(c) documents of title may be delivered through customary banking channels. (5A Del. C. 1953, § 2-308; 55 Del. Laws, c. 349.)

RULE §2-308: Absence of Specified Place for Delivery:

When Seller is not required or authorized to deliver goods through a Carrier (as in §2-504), the place for delivery shall be (unless otherwise agreed):

(a) The Seller's place of business (or if he has none, his residence)

(b) <u>Contracts for Identified Goods:</u> at the place where the identified goods were located at the time of the contract if:

1. The contract is for the sale of identified goods; and

2. At the time the contract was created, the parties knew that the identified goods were in some place other than Seller's place

(c) <u>Contracts Calling for Delivery of Documents:</u> Documents of title may be delivered through customary banking channels.

§ 2-309. Absence of specific time provisions; notice of termination.

(1) The time for shipment or delivery or any other action under a contract if not provided in this Article or agreed upon shall be a reasonable time.

(2) Where the contract provides for successive performances but is indefinite in duration it is valid for a reasonable time but unless otherwise agreed may be terminated at any time by either party.

(3) Termination of a contract by one party except on the happening of an agreed event requires that reasonable notification be received by the other party and an agreement dispensing with notification is invalid if its operation would be unconscionable. (5A Del. C. 1953, § 2-309; 55 Del. Laws, c. 349.)

RULE §2-309: Absence of Specified Time Provisions:

(1) Implied Reasonable Time: The time for shipment or delivery (or any other action under a contract) shall be a "reasonable time" (unless otherwise agreed upon or provided for in this Article).

(2) Termination of Contracts With Indefinite Duration:
- ***a. A contract will be valid for a reasonable time if:***
  - ***1. It provides for successive performances; and***
  - ***2. It is indefinite in duration***
- ***b. Such a contract, however, may be terminated at any time by either party (unless otherwise agreed).***

(3) Termination of a Contract by One Party:
- ***a. A party terminating the contract must offer the other party a reasonable notification of termination (which must actually be received by the other party to be effective) if:***
  - ***1. Only one party terminates the contract; and***
  - ***2. The termination is not the result of the occurrence of an agreed upon event.***
- ***b. An agreement waiving such notification of termination is invalid if its use would be unconscionable.***

§ 2-310. Open time for payment or running of credit; authority to ship under reservation.

Unless otherwise agreed

(a) payment is due at the time and place at which the buyer is to receive the goods even though the place of shipment is the place of delivery; and

(b) if the seller is authorized to send the goods he may ship them under reservation, and may tender the documents of title, but the buyer may inspect the goods after their arrival before payment is due unless such inspection is inconsistent with the terms of the contract (Section 2-513); and

(c) if delivery is authorized and made by way of documents of title otherwise than by subsection (b) then payment is due at the time and place at which the buyer is to receive the documents regardless of where the goods are to be received; and

(d) where the seller is required or authorized to ship the goods on credit the credit period runs from the time of shipment but post-dating the invoice or delaying its dispatch will correspondingly delay the starting of the credit period. (5A Del. C. 1953, § 2-310; 55 Del. Laws, c. 349.)

RULE §2-310: Open Time for Payment or Running of Credit; Authority to Ship Under Reservation:

(a) When Payment is Due: Unless otherwise agreed, payment is due at the time and place at which the Buyer is to receive the goods (not at the point of delivery, except as in §2-310(c))

(b) Shipment by Reservation:

1. ***If the Seller is authorized to send the goods, he may ship them under Reservation (unless otherwise agreed)***
2. ***If the Goods are Shipped under Reservation:***
    a. ***The Seller may tender the Documents of title***
    b. ***The Buyer may inspect the goods after their arrival and before payment is due (unless such inspection is inconsistent with the terms of the contract (see §2-513))***

(c) Delivering Documents of Title: Unless otherwise agreed, if delivery is authorized and made by delivering Documents of Title, then payment is due at the time and place where the Buyer is to receive the Documents (regardless of where the goods are to be received).

(d) Shipment on Credit:

1) ***If the Seller is authorized or required to ship the goods on credit, the credit-period normally begins from the time of Shipment (unless otherwise agreed).***
2) ***Extended Credit Period: The starting date of the credit***

period may be delayed by:
a) Post-dating the invoice; or
b) Delaying the dispatch of the invoice

§ 2-311. Options and cooperation respecting performance.

(1) An agreement for sale which is otherwise sufficiently definite (subsection (3) of Section 2-204) to be a contract is not made invalid by the fact that it leaves particulars of performance to be specified by one of the parties. Any such specification must be made in good faith and within limits set by commercial reasonableness.

(2) Unless otherwise agreed specifications relating to assortment of the goods are at the buyer's option and except as otherwise provided in subsections (1) (c) and (3) of Section 2-319 specifications or arrangements relating to shipment are at the seller's option.

(3) Where such specification would materially affect the other party's performance but is not seasonably made or where one party's cooperation is necessary to the agreed performance of the other but is not seasonably forthcoming, the other party in addition to all other remedies

(a) is excused for any resulting delay in his own performance; and

(b) may also either proceed to perform in any reasonable manner or after the time for a material part of his own performance treat the failure to specify or to cooperate as a breach by failure to deliver or accept the goods. (5A Del. C. 1953, § 2-311; 55 Del. Laws, c. 349.)

RULE §2-311: Options and Cooperation Respecting Performance:

(1) Details of Performance Absent:

a) An agreement for Sale (which is otherwise sufficiently definite to be considered a contract under §2-204(3)) Will not be invalidated if it leaves particular details of performance to be specified by one of the parties.
b) Any such details must be made in Good Faith, and within the limits set by "commercial reasonableness".

(2) Parties Specifying Details:

Unless otherwise agreed, the following details may be decided by certain parties:

a. <u>The Buyer</u> may decide how to assort the goods (ex: Buyer may request that each 1 dozen package of colored ice cream cones contain 4 red cones, 2 blue. cones, 3 green cones and 3 yellow cones).

b. <u>The Seller</u> may decide the details and arrangements of Shipping (except as provided for in §2-319(1)(c) and §2-319(3)).

(3) Remedies for Neglect:

i) A party may be eligible for §2-311 Remedies if:

a) <u>The Other Party Fails To Make Specifications</u> (as per §2-311(2)) - Remedies will be available if:

1. The other party's specifications would materially affect performance; and

2. The other party neglects to seasonably make such specifications (ex: The Buyer was to tell the Seller whether to ship goods by UPS or Federal Express by July 1st, but neglected to do so).

or b) <u>The Other Party Fails to Cooperate</u> - Remedies will be available if:

1. The other party's cooperation is necessary to the agreed performance; and

2. The other party does not seasonably cooperate

ii) <u>Available Remedies:</u> In such situations, the non-neglectful party:

(a) Is excused for any resulting default in his own performance (in addition to all other remedies); and

(b) May also either:

1. Proceed to perform in any reasonable manner; or

2. Treat the failure to cooperate or specify as a breach (by failure to deliver or accept goods upon his performance) after the time for a material part of his own performance

§ 2-312. Warranty of title and against infringement; buyer's obligation against infringement.

(1) Subject to subsection (2) there is in a contract for sale a warranty by the seller that

(a) the title conveyed shall be good, and its transfer rightful; and

(b) the goods shall be delivered free from any security interest or other lien or encumbrance of which the buyer at the time of contracting has no knowledge.

(2) A warranty under subsection (1) will be excluded or modified only by specific language or by circumstances which give the buyer reason to know that the person selling does not claim title in himself or that he is purporting to sell only such right or title as he or a third person may have.

(3) Unless otherwise agreed a seller who is a merchant regularly dealing in goods of the kind warrants that the goods shall be delivered free of the rightful claim of any third person by way of infringement or the like but a buyer who furnishes specifications to the seller must hold the seller harmless against any such claim which arises out of compliance with the specifications. (5A Del. C. 1953, § 2-312; 55 Del. Laws, c. 349.)

RULE §2-312: Warranty of Title:

(1) In a contract of sale, the Seller makes the following Warranties (subject to §2-312(2)):

- ***(a) Good Title:***
  - ***1. The title conveyed shall be good; and***
  - ***2. The transfer is rightful***
- ***(b) Goods Free of Liens: The goods are delivered free from Security Interests or other liens (or encumbrances) which the Buyer had no knowledge of at the time the contract was created.***

(2) Modification or Exclusion: A Warranty of Title may only be modified or excluded by:

- ***a) Specific language in the contract***
- ***b) Circumstances which give the Buyer reason to know that:***

1. The Seller does not claim title in himself; or
2. The Seller is only purporting to sell the rights which he (or a third person) may have in the goods (ex: Seller sells goods "as is").

(3) Goods Do Not Infringe Third Party Rights - Merchant Only: The Seller warrants that the goods do not infringe a third party's rights and will be delivered free from the rightful claim of any third person (ex: free from a patent or copyright infringement) if:
a) The Seller is a Merchant regularly dealing in goods of the kind sold; and
b) The infringement does not arise out of the Seller's compliance with the Buyer's instructions (ex: Buyer tells Seller to apply a label which infringes an already existing copyrighted label to its goods).

§ 2-313. Express warranties by affirmation, promise, description, sample.

(1) Express warranties by the seller are created as follows:

(a) Any affirmation of fact or promise made by the seller to the buyer which relates to the goods and becomes part of the basis of the bargain creates an express warranty that the goods shall conform to the affirmation or promise.

(b) Any description of the goods which is made part of the basis of the bargain creates an express warranty that the goods shall conform to the description.

(c) Any sample or model which is made part of the basis of the bargain creates an express warranty that the whole of the goods shall conform to the sample or model.

(2) It is not necessary to the creation of an express warranty that the seller use formal words such as "warrant" or "guarantee" or that he have a specific intention to make a warranty, but an affirmation merely of the value of the goods or a statement purporting to be merely the seller's opinion or commendation of the goods does not create a warranty. (5A Del. C. 1953, § 2-313; 55 Del. Laws, c. 349.)

RULE §2-313 - Express Warranty by Affirmation:

(1) Express Warranties by the Seller are created as follows:

(a) Warranty That Goods Shall Conform to an Affirmation or Promise - Created by any affirmation of fact or promise:
1. Which is made by the Seller to the Buyer; and
2. Relating to the goods; and
3. Which becomes a significant part of the basis of the bargain

(b) Warranty That The Goods Shall Conform to their Description - Created when any description of the goods becomes a significant factor in the basis of the bargain.

(c) Warranty That Goods Shall Conform to Sample or Model - Created when a sample or model becomes a significant factor in the basis of the bargain.

(2) Substance Over Form

a. It is not necessary for Seller to use formal words such as "warrant" or "guarantee" to create an Express Warranty

b. The following do not alone create express warranties:
1. An Affirmation merely of the value of the goods; or
2. A Statement purporting to be merely the Seller's opinion; or
3. Compliments or Commendations of the goods (ex: "Sales Puff")

§ 2-314. Implied warranty; merchantability; usage of trade.

(1) Unless excluded or modified (Section 2-316), a warranty that the goods shall be merchantable is implied in a contract for their sale if the seller is a merchant with respect to goods of that kind. Under this section the serving for value of food or drink to be consumed either on the premises or elsewhere is a sale.

(2) Goods to be merchantable must be at least such as

(a) pass without objection in the trade under the contract description; and

(b) in the case of fungible goods, are of fair average quality within the description; and

(c) are fit for the ordinary purposes for which such goods are used; and

(d) run, within the variations permitted by the agreement, of even kind, quality and quantity within each unit and among all units involved; and

(e) are adequately contained, packaged, and labeled as the agreement may require; and

(f) conform to the promises or affirmations of fact made on the container or label if any.

(3) Unless excluded or modified (Section 2-316) other implied warranties may arise from course of dealing or usage of trade. (5A Del. C. 1953, § 2-314; 55 Del. Laws, c. 349.)

RULE §2-314: Implied Warranty of Merchantability:

(1) Implied Warranty:

- ***a. A Warranty that the goods shall be merchantable is implied in a contract for their sale if:***
    - ***1. The Seller is a Merchant, selling goods of the kind sold; and***
    - ***2. There is no clause excluding or modifying such a Warranty (as per §2-316)***
- ***b. The serving of food or drink for value (regardless of where it is consumed) is considered a sale for purposes of this section.***

(2) Warranty of Merchantability: Under the Warranty of Merchantability, the Seller warrants:

- ***(a) <u>Goods Fit Trade Description</u> - Goods must pass without objection in the trade under the contract description (ex: if in order to be considered Orange Juice, a drink must contain 75% juice from oranges,***

the contents of an "Orange Juice" container must be 75% juice from oranges); and

(b) Quality - Fungible Goods must be of fair, average quality (within the description of such goods); and

(c) Fitness - Must be fit for the ordinary purposes for which such goods are used (for particular purposes, see §2-315); and

(d) Uniformity - They must have similar quality and Characteristics (within variations permitted by the agreement) Within each unit, and among all units involved in the contract; and

(e) Packaging - The goods must be adequately contained, packaged, and labeled (as the agreement or nature of the product may require (ex: pills to be sold over the counter should be packaged in tamper-proof containers)); and

(f) Goods Fit Package Description - Must conform to the Promise or Affirmations made on the container or label.

(3) Other implied warranties may arise from the Course of Dealing or Usage of Trade (unless excluded or modified as per §2-316)

§ 2-315. Implied warranty; fitness for particular purpose.

Where the seller at the time of contracting has reason to know any particular purpose for which the goods are required and that the buyer is relying on the seller's skill or judgment to select or furnish suitable goods, there is unless excluded or modified under the next section an implied warranty that the goods shall be fit for such purpose. (5A Del. C. 1953, § 2-315; 55 Del. Laws, c. 349.)

RULE §2-315: Implied Warranty of Fitness for a Particular Purpose:

The Seller impliedly promises the Buyer that the goods shall be fit for a particular purpose if:

a) At the time the contract was created, the Seller had reason to know any particular purpose for which Buyer wanted to use the goods; and
b) The Buyer relied on the Seller's skill or judgment to select or furnish suitable goods; and
c) Such a warranty has not been excluded or modified (as per §2-316)

§ 2-316. Exclusion or modification of warranties.

(1) Words or conduct relevant to the creation of an express warranty and words or conduct tending to negate or limit warranty shall be construed wherever reasonable as consistent with each other; but subject to the provisions of this Article on parol or extrinsic evidence (Section 2-202) negation or limitation is inoperative to the extent that such construction is unreasonable.

(2) Subject to subsection (3), to exclude or modify the implied warranty of merchantability or any part of it the language must mention merchantability and in case of a writing must be conspicuous, and to exclude or modify any implied warranty of fitness the exclusion must be by a writing and conspicuous. Language to exclude all implied warranties of fitness is sufficient if it states, for example, that "There are no warranties which extend beyond the description on the face hereof."

(3) Notwithstanding subsection (2)

(a) unless the circumstances indicate otherwise, all implied warranties are excluded by expressions like "as is", "with all faults" or other language which in common understanding calls the buyer's attention to the exclusion of warranties and makes plain that there is no implied warranty; and

(b) when the buyer before entering into the contract has examined the goods or the sample or model as fully as he desired or has refused to examine the goods there is no implied warranty with regard to defects which an examination ought in the circumstances to have revealed to him; and

(c) an implied warranty can also be excluded or modified by course of dealing or course of performance or usage of trade.

(4) Remedies for breach of warranty can be limited in accordance with the provisions of this Article on liquidation or limitation of damages and on contractual modification of remedy (Sections 2-718 and 2-719).

(5) The implied warranties of merchantability and fitness shall not be applicable to a contract for the sale of human blood, blood plasma or other human tissue or organs from a blood bank or reservoir of such other tissues or organs. Such blood, blood plasma or tissue or organs shall not for the purposes of this Article be considered commodities or goods subject to sale or barter, but shall be considered as medical services. (5A Del. C. 1953, § 2-316; 55 Del. Laws, c. 349; 55 Del. Laws, c. 391.)

RULE §2-316: Exclusion or Modification of Warranties:

(1) Consistent Construction of Words and Conduct:

- ***a. The following shall be construed consistently whenever possible:***
    - ***1. Words or Conduct relating to the creation of an Express Warranty***
    - ***2. Words or Conduct tending to negate or limit such warranties***
- ***b. Negation or Limitation of such warranties are invalid to the extent that a consistent construction is unreasonable (subject to §2-202 (Parole Evidence)).***

(2) Requirements of Excluding or Modifying Implied Warranties (subject to §2-316(3)):

- ***a. To Exclude or Modify an Implied Warranty of Merchantability:***
    - ***1. The language must mention merchantability; and***
    - ***2. The language must be conspicuous if in writing***
- ***b. To Exclude or Modify an Implied Warranty of Fitness:***
    - ***1. The exclusion must be in writing; and***
    - ***2. The language must be conspicuous***
- ***c. To Exclude ALL Implied Warranties of Fitness: Language must be very clear (ex: "There are no warranties which extend beyond the description on the face hereof").***

(3) Rules Regarding Excluding Implied Warranties: Notwithstanding §2-316(2) (above):

- ***(a) All implied warranties may be excluded by the use of language which, in common understanding:***

1) Calls the Buyer's attention to the exclusion of Warranties; and
2) Makes it clear that there are no implied warranties (unless the circumstances indicate otherwise (ex: sold "as is" or "with all faults"))

(b) Buyer's Inspection: Implied Warranties will be limited to defects which the Buyer should have reasonably discovered (under the circumstances) if:
1. The Buyer inspects (to his satisfaction) the goods or a sample model before entering into the contract; or
2. The Buyer refuses to examine the goods

(c) An Implied Warranty can also be Excluded or Modified by:
1) The Course of Dealing (as per §1-205); or
2) The Course of Performance (as per §2-208); or
3) The Usage of Trade (as per §1-205)

(4) Limitations for Breach of Warranty: Remedies for breach of warranty may be limited in accordance with the provisions dealing with:
a) Liquidation or Limitation of Damages (§2-718)
b) Contractual Modification of Remedy (§2-719)

§ 2-317. Cumulation and conflict of warranties express or implied.

Warranties whether express or implied shall be construed as consistent with each other and as cumulative, but if such construction is unreasonable the intention of the parties shall determine which warranty is dominant. In ascertaining that intention the following rules apply:

(a) Exact or technical specifications displace an inconsistent sample or model or general language of description.

(b) A sample from an existing bulk displaces inconsistent general language of description.

(c) Express warranties displace inconsistent implied warranties other than an implied warranty of fitness for a particular purpose. (5A Del. C. 1953, § 2-317; 55 Del. Laws, c. 349.)

RULE §2-317: Cumulation and Conflict of Implied or Express Warranties:

1. Warranties (whether express or implied) shall be construed to be cumulative and consistent with each other, whenever reasonable.

2. If such a construction is unreasonable, the intention of the parties shall determine which warranty is dominant.

3. Rules in Determining the Intention of the Parties (with regard to conflicting warranties):
(a) Exact or Technical Specifications of the Goods displace an inconsistent sample, model, or general language of the goods' description.
(b) A Sample From An Existing Bulk displaces inconsistent general language or description of the goods.
(c) An Express Warranty displaces inconsistent, implied warranties (other than the implied warranty of fitness for a particular purpose (§2-315)).

§ 2-318. Third party beneficiaries of warranties express or implied.

A seller's warranty whether express or implied extends to any natural person who may reasonably be expected to use, consume or be affected by the goods and who is injured by breach of the warranty. A seller may not exclude or limit the operation of this section. (5A Del. C. 1953, § 2-318; 55 Del. Laws, c. 349.)

RULE §2-318: Third Party Beneficiaries of Warranties:

This section shall be omitted if The United States Congress adopts it (as of 1995 it has not).

ALTERNATIVE A
1. A Seller's express or implied warranties extend to:

a) Any natural person in the Buyer's family or household; and
b) Any guest in the Buyer's home

2. The Seller will be held responsible for breach of warranty to the third party if:
a) It is reasonable to expect such a person to use, consume, or be affected by the goods (ex: A Seller should expect a third party to sit on a Buyer's dining room chair, but the Seller probably would not expect a third party to use the Buyer's dishwasher); and
b) b) That person is injured by the breach of the warranty.

3. The Seller may not exclude or limit the warranties to third persons.

ALTERNATIVE B

1. A Seller's express and implied warranties extend to any natural person in the Buyer's family or household if:
a) It is reasonable to expect such a person to use, consume, or be affected by the goods; and
b) That person is injured by the breach of the warranty.

2. The Seller may not exclude or limit its liability to third persons.

ALTERNATIVE C

1. A Seller's express and implied warranties extends to any person if:
a) It is reasonable to expect such a person to use, consume, or be affected by the goods; and
b) That person is injured by the breach of the warranty.

2. The Seller may not exclude or limit its liability to third persons if the warranty is meant to extend to that person.

§ 2-319. F.O.B. and F.A.S. terms.

(1) Unless otherwise agreed the term F.O.B. (which means "free on board") at a named place, even though used only in connection with the stated price, is a delivery term under which

(a) when the term is F.O.B. the place of shipment, the seller must at that place ship the goods in the manner provided in this Article (Section 2-504) and bear the expense and risk of putting them into the possession of the carrier; or

(b) when the term is F.O.B. the place of destination, the seller must at his own expense and risk transport the goods to that place and there tender delivery of them in the manner provided in this Article (Section 2-503);

(c) when under either (a) or (b) the term is also F.O.B. vessel, car or other vehicle, the seller must in addition at his own expense and risk load the goods on board. If the term is F.O.B. vessel the buyer must name the vessel and in an appropriate case the seller must comply with the provisions of this Article on the form of bill of lading (Section 2-323).

(2) Unless otherwise agreed the term F.A.S. vessel (which means "free alongside") at a named port, even though used only in connection with the stated price, is a delivery term under which the seller must

(a) at his own expense and risk deliver the goods alongside the vessel in the manner usual in that port or on a dock designated and provided by the buyer; and

(b) obtain and tender a receipt for the goods in exchange for which the carrier is under a duty to issue a bill of lading.

(3) Unless otherwise agreed in any case falling within subsection (1) (a) or (c) or subsection (2) the buyer must seasonably give any needed instructions for making delivery, including when the term is F.A.S. or F.O.B. the loading berth of the vessel and in an appropriate case its name and sailing date. The seller may treat the failure of needed instructions as a failure of cooperation under this Article (Section 2-311). He may also at his option move the goods in any reasonable manner preparatory to delivery or shipment.

(4) Under the term F.O.B. vessel or F.A.S. unless otherwise agreed the buyer must make payment against tender of the required documents and the seller may not tender nor the buyer demand delivery of the goods in substitution for the documents. (5A Del. C. 1953, § 2-319; 55 Del. Laws, c. 349.)

RULE §2-319: F.O.B. and F.A.S.:

***Note:* The terms F.O.B. and F.A.S. will be construed as "Delivery Terms" even though they have been used as "Price Terms" (unless the parties agree otherwise)**

(1) "F.O.B." (Free on Board) - unless otherwise agreed, the term F.O.B. implies the following:

- ***(a) F.O.B. (Place of Shipment):***
  The Seller has the following responsibilities:
  1. ***Deliver goods to their specified place of shipment (i.e. to the Carrier's possession) (as per §2-504); and***
  2. ***Pay for the shipment; and***
  3. ***Bear the risk of putting the goods into the Carrier's possession***

- ***(b) F.O.B.(Place of Destination):***
  The Seller has the following responsibilities:
  1. ***Pay for the transport of the goods to the specified place of destination; and***
  2. ***Bear the risk of transporting the goods to their specified destination; and***
  3. ***Tender delivery of the goods to the Buyer (as per §2-503)***

- ***(c) F.O.B.(Vessel, car, other vehicle) (either under (a) or (b)):***
  1. ***Seller's Responsibility: The Seller has the following additional responsibilities:***
     - ***a. Pay for loading the goods on board***
     - ***b. Bear the risk of loading the goods on board***
     - ***c. Comply with §2-323 (regarding the form of the Bill of Lading)***
  2. ***Buyer's Responsibility: The Buyer must name the particular vessel which the goods will be loaded upon.***

(2) "F.A.S. (vessel)" (Free alongside) - unless otherwise agreed, the term F.A.S. implies that the Seller has the following

responsibilities:

(a) Pay for and bear the risk of either:

1) Delivering the goods alongside the vessel (in the manner usual in that port; or

2) Delivering the goods on a dock designated and provided by Buyer

and (b) Obtain and Tender a receipt for the goods, in which the Carrier promises to issue a BOL

(3) Buyer's Obligation to Instruct Seller

a) The Buyer must seasonably give any needed instructions for delivery (unless otherwise agreed in an FAS, FOB (shipment), or FOB(vessel) contract), including:

1. The loading berth of the vessel (if the terms are FOB or FAS)

2. The name of the ship and its sailing date (in appropriate cases)

b) <u>Buyer's Failure to Instruct</u> - If the Buyer fails to seasonably give the Seller the appropriate shipping instructions:

1. The Seller may treat Buyer's failure to give instructions as a Failure to Cooperate (as per §2-311); and

2. The Seller may, at his option, move the goods in any reasonable manner in preparation for delivery or shipment.

(4) Tender of Documents for FAS and FOB(vessel) Contracts:

a. The Buyer must make payment against tender of the required documents under an FOB(vessel) or FAS shipping contract (unless otherwise agreed).

b. The Buyer may not demand delivery of the goods, nor may the Seller tender goods, in substitution of the documents.

§ 2-320. C.I.F. and C. & F. terms.

(1) The term C.I.F. means that the price includes in a lump sum the cost of the goods and the insurance and freight to the named destination. The term C. & F. or C.F. means that the price so includes cost and freight to the named destination.

(2) Unless otherwise agreed and even though used only in connection with the stated price and destination, the term C.I.F. destination or its equivalent requires the seller at his own expense and risk to

(a) put the goods into the possession of a carrier at the port for shipment and obtain a negotiable bill or bills of lading covering the entire transportation to the named destination; and

(b) load the goods and obtain a receipt from the carrier (which may be contained in the bill of lading) showing that the freight has been paid or provided for; and

(c) obtain a policy or certificate of insurance, including any war risk insurance, of a kind and on terms then current at the port of shipment in the usual amount, in the currency of the contract, shown to cover the same goods covered by the bill of lading and providing for payment of loss to the order of the buyer or for the account of whom it may concern; but the seller may add to the price the amount of the premium for any such war risk insurance; and

(d) prepare an invoice of the goods and procure any other documents required to effect shipment or to comply with the contract; and

(e) forward and tender with commercial promptness all the documents in due form and with any indorsement necessary to perfect the buyer's rights.

(3) Unless otherwise agreed the term C. & F. or its equivalent has the same effect and imposes upon the seller the same obligation and risks as a C.I.F. term except the obligation as to insurance.

(4) Under the term C.I.F. or C. & F. unless otherwise agreed the buyer must make payment against tender of the required documents and the seller may not tender nor the buyer demand delivery of the goods in substitution for the documents. (5A Del. C. 1953, § 2-320; 55 Del. Laws, c. 349.)

RULE §2-320: C.I.F. & C.& F.:

(1) Definitions:

a) "C.I.F." means that the Price includes:
1. The cost of the Goods; and
2. The Insurance; and
3. The Freight (to the named destination)

b) "C&F" means that the Price includes:
1. The cost of the Goods; and
2. The Freight (to the named destination)

(2) The Term "C. I. F. (destination)" (or its equivalent) implies that the Seller shall have the following responsibilities (unless otherwise agreed):

(a)
1. Pay for putting the goods into possession of the Carrier (at the port for shipment); and
2. Bear the risk of putting the goods into possession of the Carrier (at the port for shipment); and
3. Obtain a Negotiable Bill of Lading covering the goods; and

(b)
1. Load the goods; and
2. Obtain a receipt from the Carrier (may be part of the BOL) showing that freight has been paid/provided for; and

(c) Obtain a policy or certify insurance (including war Risk Insurance)
1. The insurance must be of the type typical at the port of shipment
2. The insurance contract must cover the goods in the BOL
3. The beneficiary must be the Buyer or "whom it may concern"
4. War risk premiums may be added to CIF price

and (d) Prepare an invoice of the goods and procure any other documents required to effect shipment (or to comply

with the contract)

and (e) Forward and Tender all documents

1. With Commercial Promptness

2. In Due Form

3. With any necessary indorsements to perfect the Buyer's rights

(3) Unless otherwise agreed, C&F has the same effect and obligations as a CIF contract, except for the insurance obligations.

(4) The Buyer must make payment against tender of the required Documents (unless otherwise agreed) under CIF and C&F contracts.

§ 2-321. C.I.F. or C. & F.: "net landed weights"; "payment on arrival"; warranty of condition on arrival.

Under a contract containing a term C.I.F. or C. & F.

(1) Where the price is based on or is to be adjusted according to "net landed weights", "delivered weights", "out turn" quantity or quality or the like, unless otherwise agreed the seller must reasonably estimate the price. The payment due on tender of the documents called for by the contract is the amount so estimated, but after final adjustment of the price a settlement must be made with commercial promptness.

(2) An agreement described in subsection (1) or any warranty of quality or condition of the goods on arrival places upon the seller the risk of ordinary deterioration, shrinkage and the like in transportation but has no effect on the place or time of identification to the contract for sale or delivery or on the passing of the risk of loss.

(3) Unless otherwise agreed where the contract provides for payment on or after arrival of the goods the seller must before payment allow such preliminary inspection as is feasible; but if the goods are lost delivery of the documents and payment are due when the goods should have arrived. (5A Del. C. 1953, § 2-321; 55 Del. Laws, c. 349.)

RULE §2-321: C.I.F. or C&F: "Net Landed Weight"; "Payments on Arrival"; Warranty of Condition on Arrival:

This Section applies to contracts containing CIF or C&F terms.

(1) Price Based on Landed Weight

a. The Seller must reasonably estimate the price if it is to be based on or adjusted according to its weight or quality (unless otherwise agreed).

b. Sales based on quality or weight upon delivery are often denoted with such terms as:

1. "Net Landed Weight"

2. "Delivered Weights"

3. "Out turn" quality or quantity of the goods

c. <u>Payment Due:</u> The amount due on tender of the documents is the amount initially estimated by the Seller.

d. After final price adjustments are made, a settlement for the balance must be made with commercial promptness.

(2) Risk of Deterioration

a) The Seller shall have the <u>Risk of Ordinary Deterioration and Shrinkage</u> (and the like) while the goods are in transit if:

1) An agreement (as described in (1) above) has been created (basing the price on the weight or quality of the goods upon delivery); or

2) A warranty of quality or condition of the goods on arrival has been created

b) Such agreements have no effect on:

1) The place or time of identification of goods to the contract (for sale or delivery); or

2) The passing of risk of loss

(3) Time For Payment

a. <u>Inspection Before Payment:</u> The Seller must allow a preliminary inspection ("as feasible") of the goods before the Buyer makes payment if the contract allows payment

to be made on or after the arrival of the goods (unless otherwise agreed).

b. <u>Lost Goods:</u> Delivery of the documents and payment are due when the goods would have arrived if the goods are lost.

§ 2-322. Delivery "ex-ship."

(1) Unless otherwise agreed a term for delivery of goods "ex-ship" (which means from the carrying vessel) or in equivalent language is not restricted to a particular ship and requires delivery from a ship which has reached a place at the named port of destination where goods of the kind are usually discharged.

(2) Under such a term unless otherwise agreed

(a) the seller must discharge all liens arising out of the carriage and furnish the buyer with a direction which puts the carrier under a duty to deliver the goods; and

(b) the risk of loss does not pass to the buyer until the goods leave the ship's tackle or are otherwise properly unloaded. (5A Del. C. 1953, § 2-322; 55 Del. Laws, c. 349.)

RULE §2-322: Delivery "Ex-Ship":

(1) "EX-SHIP" (or equivalent language) means (unless otherwise agreed):

a. That goods need not be delivered on a particular ship; and

b. Delivery will be made from a ship which has reached a place at the named port of destination (where goods of that kind are usually discharged).

(2) Obligations under "Ex-Ship" Terms:

(a) <u>The Seller must:</u>

1. Discharge all liens which arise out of carriage; and

2. Furnish the Buyer with a direction that obligates the Carrier to deliver the goods

(b) <u>Risk of Loss:</u> The Risk of Loss passes to the Buyer when:

1. The goods leave the ship's tackle; or

2. The goods are otherwise properly unloaded from the ship

§ 2-323. Form of bill of lading required in overseas shipment; "overseas."

(1) Where the contract contemplates overseas shipment and contains a term C.I.F. or C. & F. or F.O.B. vessel, the seller unless otherwise agreed must obtain negotiable bill of lading stating that the goods have been loaded on board or, in the case of a term C.I.F. or C. & F., received for shipment.

(2) Where in a case within subsection (1) a bill of lading has been issued in a set of parts, unless otherwise agreed if the documents are not to be sent from abroad the buyer may demand tender of the full set; otherwise only one part of the bill of lading need be tendered. Even if the agreement expressly requires a full set

(a) due tender of a single part is acceptable within the provisions of this Article on cure of improper delivery (subsection (1) of Section 2-508); and

(b) even though the full set is demanded, if the documents are sent from abroad the person tendering an incomplete set may nevertheless require payment upon furnishing an indemnity which the buyer in good faith deems adequate.

(3) A shipment by water or by air or a contract contemplating such shipment is "overseas" insofar as by usage of trade or agreement it is subject to the commercial, financing or shipping practices characteristic of international deep water commerce. (5A Del. C. 1953, § 2-323; 55 Del. Laws, c. 349.)

RULE §2-323: Bill of Lading:

(1) Requirements of the Bill of Lading
- ***a. The Seller must obtain a <u>Negotiable Bill of Lading</u> (unless otherwise agreed) if:***
  - ***1. The contract involves an overseas shipment; and***
  - ***2. The terms are FOB(vessel), CIF or C&F b. <u>Contents of the Negotiable Bill of Lading:</u>***
    - ***1. FOB - must state that goods have been loaded on board.***
    - ***2. CIF or C&F - must state that the goods have been received for shipment.***

(2) Multi-Part Documents

i) When a Bill of Lading has been issued in a <u>set of parts,</u> only one part need be tendered unless:

a) The agreement expressly requires a full set to be tendered; or

b) <u>Both:</u>

1. The Buyer demands a full set to be tendered; and

2. The documents are not to be sent from abroad

ii) <u>The following rules apply even if the contract expressly requires a full set of documents to be tendered:</u>

a) Due tender of a single part of the BOL is acceptable to cure improper delivery (as per §2-508(1)); and

b) <u>Documents sent from abroad:</u> If the documents are sent from abroad, the person tendering an incomplete set of documents may require payment upon furnishing an <u>indemnity</u> (which the Buyer deems to have been made in good faith), even if the full set is demanded.

(3) "Overseas" - an "overseas" contract or shipment is one:

a) Involving shipment by <u>water</u> or air; and

b) That is subject to commercial, financial, or shipping practices characteristic of international deep water commerce, either by Usage of Trade or Agreement.

§ 2-324. "No arrival, no sale" term.

Under a term "no arrival, no sale" or terms of like meaning, unless otherwise agreed,

(a) the seller must properly ship conforming goods and if they arrive by any means he must tender them on arrival but he assumes no obligation that the goods will arrive unless he has caused the non-arrival; and

(b) where without fault of the seller the goods are in part lost or have so deteriorated as no longer to conform to the contract or arrive after the contract time, the buyer may proceed as if there had been casualty to identified goods (Section 2-613). (5A Del. C. 1953, § 2-324; 55 Del. Laws, c. 349.)

RULE §2-324: "No Arrival, No Sale" Term:

The following sections govern the use of the term "No Arrival, No Sale" or terms of similar meaning (unless otherwise agreed):

(a) Obligations of the Seller:
- ***1. The Seller must:***
  - ***a. Properly ship conforming goods***
  - ***b. Tender the goods on arrival (if they arrive by any means)***
- ***2. <u>The Seller's Risk:</u> the Seller assumes no obligation that the goods will arrive, unless he has caused their non-arrival.***

(b) Buyer's Remedy: The Buyer may proceed as if there had been Casualty to Identified Goods (as per §2-613) if:
- ***1. The Seller is not at fault; and***
- ***2. <u>Either:</u>***
  - ***a. Some of the goods are lost; or***
  - ***b. The goods have deteriorated (so as to no longer conform to the contract); or***
  - ***c. The goods arrive after the contract time***

§ 2-325. "Letter of credit" term; "confirmed credit."

(1) Failure of the buyer seasonably to furnish an agreed letter of credit is a breach of the contract for sale.

(2) The delivery to seller of a proper letter of credit suspends the buyer's obligation to pay. If the letter of credit is dishonored, the seller may on seasonable notification to the buyer require payment directly from him.

(3) Unless otherwise agreed the term "letter of credit" or "banker's credit" in a contract for sale means an irrevocable credit issued by a financing agency of good repute

and, where the shipment is overseas, of good international repute. The term "confirmed credit" means that the credit must also carry the direct obligation of such an agency which does business in the seller's financial market. (5A Del. C. 1953, § 2-325; 55 Del. Laws, c. 349.)

RULE §2-325: Letter of Credit:

(1) Failure of a Buyer to seasonably provide an agreed Letter of Credit is a breach of the contract for sale.

(2) L/C as Payment:

a) The delivery of a proper L/C to the Seller suspends the Buyer's obligation to pay.

b) If the L/C is dishonored, the Seller may require payment directly from Buyer upon seasonable notification.

(3) Definitions:

a) "Letter of Credit" (or "banker's credit") - means (unless otherwise agreed) an irrevocable credit issued by a financing agency of good repute.

b) "Confirmed Credit" - means that the credit carries the direct obligation of a financing agency which does business in the Seller's financial market.

§ 2-326. Sale on approval and sale or return; rights of creditors.

(1) Unless otherwise agreed, if delivered goods may be returned by the buyer even though they conform to the contract, the transaction is

(a) a "sale on approval" if the goods are delivered primarily for use, and

(b) a "sale or return" if the goods are delivered primarily for resale.

(2) Goods held on approval are not subject to the claims of the buyer's creditors until acceptance; goods held on sale or return are subject to such claims while in the buyer's possession.

(3) Any "or return" term of a contract for sale is to be treated as a separate contract for sale within the statute of frauds section of this Article (Section 2-201) and as contradicting the sale aspect of the contract within the provisions of this Article on parol or extrinsic evidence (Section 2-202). (5A Del. C. 1953, § 2-326; 55 Del. Laws, c. 349; 72 Del. Laws, c. 401, § 8.)

RULE §2-326: Consignment:

(1) If delivered goods may be returned by the Buyer (even though they conform), the transaction is considered either:
- ***(a) A "Sale on Approval" - if the goods are delivered primarily for use (ex: trial period); or***
- ***(b) A "Sale or Return" - if the goods are delivered primarily for resale***

(2) Effect of Classification (subject to (3) below):
- ***(a) "Sale on Approval" goods are not subject to claims of the Buyer's creditors until goods are accepted***
- ***(b) "Sale or Return" goods are subject to claims of the Buyer' creditors while in the "Buyer's" possession***

(3) <u>"Sale or Return"</u>
- ***i) Goods are deemed to be "Sale or Return" if:***
  - ***a) Goods are delivered to a person for the purpose of resale; and***
  - ***b) The person (Consignee) maintains a place of business (where he deals in goods of the kind involved); and***
  - ***c) The Consignee sells the goods under a name other than the name of the person making the delivery (i.e. the Consignor).***
- ***ii) Form over Substance: These provisions apply even if:***
  - ***a) Title is agreed not to pass until payment or resale; or***
  - ***b) The contract uses words such as "on consignment" or "on memorandum"***
- ***iii) <u>EXCEPTIONS to "Sale or Return" Classification</u>:***
  - ***(a) The person making the delivery complies with an***

applicable law providing for Consignor's interests to be evidenced by a sign; or

(b) The person making delivery establishes that the person conducting business is known by creditors to be "substantially engaged in selling the goods of others" (ex: a known auction house); or

(c) The person making delivery complies with filing provisions of Article 9.

(4) Any "or return" term of a contract for sale is considered:

(a) A separate contract for sale within the Statute of Frauds (§2-204); and

(b) To be contradicting the sale aspect of the contract (within the provisions for Parol or Extrinsic Evidence (as per §2-202))

§ 2-327. Special incidents of sale on approval and sale or return.

(1) Under a sale on approval unless otherwise agreed

(a) although the goods are identified to the contract the risk of loss and the title do not pass to the buyer until acceptance; and

(b) use of the goods consistent with the purpose of trial is not acceptance but failure seasonably to notify the seller of election to return the goods is acceptance, and if the goods conform to the contract acceptance of any part is acceptance of the whole; and

(c) after due notification of election to return, the return is at the seller's risk and expense but a merchant buyer must follow any reasonable instructions.

(2) Under a sale or return unless otherwise agreed

(a) the option to return extends to the whole or any commercial unit of the goods while in substantially their original condition, but must be exercised seasonably; and

(b) the return is at the buyer's risk and expense. (5A Del. C. 1953, § 2-327; 55 Del. Laws, c. 349.)

RULE §2-327: Special Incidents of Sale on Approval and Sale or Return:

(1) <u>Rules Governing Sales Made On "Sale or Approval"</u> (unless otherwise agreed):

- ***(a) Risk of Loss and Title: The Risk of Loss and Title pass to the Buyer upon acceptance (even if the goods are identified to the contract)***
- ***(b) Acceptance of Goods Sold on "Sale or Return"***
  1. ***Use of the goods consistent with the purpose of the trial offer is not considered acceptance***
  2. ***Failure to seasonably notify the Seller of an intention to return the goods is considered acceptance.***
  3. ***The Buyer will be deemed to have accepted all the goods under the contract if:***
     - ***a) The Buyer accepts any part of the goods under the contract; and***
     - ***b) The goods conform to the contract***
     - ***c) Returning Goods:***
       1. ***After due notification to the Seller, the return of the goods shall be at the <u>Seller's</u> risk and expense.***
       2. ***A merchant Buyer must follow any reasonable instructions of the Seller.***

(2) <u>Rules Governing Sales Made on "Sale or Return"</u> (unless otherwise agreed):

- ***(a) Apportionable: The Buyer may return all or some of the goods if:***
  1. ***They are returned seasonably; and***
  2. ***They are in substantially their original condition and***
  3. ***They are returned in commercial units***
- ***(b) Return: The <u>Buyer</u> shall bear the expense and risk of loss when returning the goods.***

§ 2-328. Sale by auction.

(1) In a sale by auction if goods are put up in lots each lot is the subject of a separate sale.

(2) A sale by auction is complete when the auctioneer so announces by the fall of the hammer or in other customary manner. Where a bid is made while the hammer is falling in acceptance of a prior bid the auctioneer may in his discretion reopen the bidding or declare the goods sold under the bid on which the hammer was falling.

(3) Such a sale is with reserve unless the goods are in explicit terms put up without reserve. In an auction with reserve the auctioneer may withdraw the goods at any time until he announces completion of the sale. In an auction without reserve, after the auctioneer calls for bids on an article or lot, that article or lot cannot be withdrawn unless no bid is made within a reasonable time. In either case a bidder may retract his bid until the auctioneer's announcement of completion of the sale, but a bidder's retraction does not revive any previous bid.

(4) If the auctioneer knowingly receives a bid on the seller's behalf or the seller makes or procures such a bid, and notice has not been given that liberty for such bidding is reserved, the buyer may at his option avoid the sale or take the goods at the price of the last good faith bid prior to the completion of the sale. This subsection shall not apply to any bid at a forced sale. (5A Del. C. 1953, § 2-328; 55 Del. Laws, c. 349.)

RULE §2-328: Sale by Auction:

(1) In a Sale by Auction where goods are put up in lots, each lot is subject to a separate sale.

(2) The Auction:

- ***a. A Sale by Auction is complete when the auctioneer so announces (by fall of the hammer or other customary manner).***
- ***b. Auctioneer's Discretion: If someone places a bid while the auctioneer's hammer is "falling", the auctioneer may:***
    - ***1. Reopen the bidding process; or***
    - ***2. Close the bidding process (and declare the goods sold to the person who bid before the hammer fell).***

(3) Reserve:

a. <u>Auction With Reserve</u> - In an auction with reserve, the auctioneer may withdraw the goods at any time before he announces the completion of the sale.

b. <u>Auction Without Reserve</u> - Once the auctioneer takes bids, the article or lot may not be withdrawn - unless there are no bids within a reasonable amount of time.

c. Goods sold by Auction are deemed to be put up for auction "with reserve ", unless it is explicitly stated that they are to be sold without reserve.

d. <u>Retracting Bids:</u>

1. A bidder may retract his bid at any time before the auctioneer announces the completion of the sale.

2. Retraction of a bid <u>does not</u> automatically revive any previous bid.

(4) <u>Buyer's Option to Avoid Sale:</u>

a. The Buyer, at his option, may avoid the sale or take the goods at the price of the last good faith bid before completion if:

1) Either:

i. The auctioneer knowingly receives a bid on the Seller's behalf; or

ii. The Seller makes or procures a bid <u>himself</u>

and 2) There has not been notice that the Seller may bid on the goods.

b. This section does not apply to any bid at a forced sale.

UNIFORM COMMERCIAL CODE

ARTICLE 2 - SALES

PART 4

Title, Creditors and Good Faith Purchases

§ 2-401. Passing of title; reservation for security; limited application of this section.

Each provision of this Article with regard to the rights, obligations and remedies of the seller, the buyer, purchasers or other third parties applies irrespective of title to the goods except where the provision refers to such title. Insofar as situations are not covered by the other provisions of this Article and matters concerning title become material the following rules apply:

(1) Title to goods cannot pass under a contract for sale prior to their identification to the contract (Section 2-501), and unless otherwise explicitly agreed the buyer acquires by their identification a special property as limited by this subtitle. Any retention or reservation by the seller of the title (property) in goods shipped or delivered to the buyer is limited in effect to a reservation of a security interest. Subject to these provisions and to the provisions of the Article on Secured Transactions (Article 9), title to goods passes from the seller to the buyer in any manner and on any conditions explicitly agreed on by the parties.

(2) Unless otherwise explicitly agreed title passes to the buyer at the time and place at which the seller completes his performance with reference to the physical delivery of the goods, despite any reservation of a security interest and even though a document of title is to be delivered at a different time or place; and in particular and despite any reservation of a security interest by the bill of lading

(a) if the contract requires or authorizes the seller to send the goods to the buyer but does not require him to deliver them at destination, title passes to the buyer at the time and place of shipment; but

(b) if the contract requires delivery at destination, title passes on tender there.

(3) Unless otherwise explicitly agreed where delivery is to be made without moving the goods,

(a) if the seller is to deliver a document of title, title passes at the time when and the place where he delivers such documents; or

(b) if the goods are at the time of contracting already identified and no documents are to be delivered, title passes at the time and place of contracting.

(4) A rejection or other refusal by the buyer to receive or retain the goods, whether or not justified, or a justified revocation of acceptance revests title to the goods in the seller. Such revesting occurs by operation of law and is not a "sale". (5A Del. C. 1953, § 2-401; 55 Del. Laws, c. 349.)

RULE §2-401: Passing of Title; Reservation for Security; Limited Application of This Section:

Preamble to §2-401 - Title Not a Consideration: ***The Provisions of Article 2 apply regardless of who has title to the goods (unless the provisions refer to such title) when they deal with the Rights, Obligations, and Remedies of:***

- ***a) A Buyer; or***
- ***b) A Seller; or***
- ***c) A Purchaser; or***
- ***d) Other third parties***

(1) Passing of Title

- ***a) The title to goods shall pass from the Seller to the Buyer according to the manner and conditions explicitly agreed upon (subject to Article 2 and Article 9 (Secured Transactions)).***
- ***b) Identification Required:*** ***Title to goods cannot pass until the goods are identified to the contract for sale (as per §2-501) (note: Future Goods cannot be the subject of a present sale).***
- ***c) Buyer's Rights Upon Identification:*** ***The Buyer will acquire a Special Property Right (as limited by this Act) in the goods once they are identified, unless the parties explicitly agree otherwise.***
- ***d) Shipment by Reservation:*** ***If a Seller ships or delivers goods under "Reservation" (i.e. he retains or reserves***

title in the goods) the Seller will have the same rights as he would if he had a Reservation of a Security Interest.

(2) Passing of Title When Goods Are Physically Delivered

i) Title passes to the Buyer at the time and place at which Seller physically delivers the goods (i.e. completes performance) to the Buyer (unless otherwise explicitly agreed upon), even if:

1. The Seller has reserved a Security Interest in the goods or

2. A Document of Title is to be delivered at a different time and place (i.e. they will not be delivered with the goods)

ii) Passing of Title in Bill of Lading Transactions:

(a) <u>Shipment Contract:</u> Title passes at the time and place of Shipment if:

1. The contract requires/authorizes the Seller to send the goods to the Buyer; and

2. The contract does not require the Seller to deliver them at their destination (ex: "FOB" - Seller only has to deliver goods to the carrier)

(b) <u>Destination Contract:</u> Title passes on tender of the goods at the specified destination if the contract requires the Seller to deliver the goods at a particular destination.

(3) Passing of Title When Goods Are To Be Delivered Without Being Moved: This section applies to transactions where delivery is to be made without moving the goods (unless otherwise agreed):

(a) <u>Delivery of Documents:</u> Title passes upon delivery of the documents of title if the Seller is to deliver them.

(b) <u>No Delivery of Documents:</u> Title passes at the time and place of contracting if:

1. The goods are identified when the contract is made and

2. No documents are to be delivered

(4) Passing of Title When Buyer Rejects:

a) Title to the goods "revests" in the Seller if:

1. The Buyer rejects or refuses to receive or retain the goods (whether or not it is justified); or

2. The Buyer properly revokes his acceptance of the goods

b) Such revesting occurs by operation of law, and is not considered a "Sale."

§ 2-402. Rights of seller's creditors against sold goods.

(1) Except as provided in subsections (2) and (3), rights of unsecured creditors of the seller with respect to goods which have been identified to a contract for sale are subject to the buyer's rights to recover the goods under this Article (Sections 2-502 and 2-716).

(2) A creditor of the seller may treat a sale or an identification of goods to a contract for sale as void if as against him a retention of possession by the seller is fraudulent under any rule of law of the state where the goods are situated, except that retention of possession in good faith and current course of trade by a merchant-seller for a commercially reasonable time after a sale or identification is not fraudulent.

(3) Nothing in this Article shall be deemed to impair the rights of creditors of the seller

(a) under the provisions of the Article on Secured Transactions (Article 9); or

(b) where identification to the contract or delivery is made not in current course of trade but in satisfaction of or as security for a pre-existing claim for money, security or the like and is made under circumstances which under any rule of law of the state where the goods are situated would apart from this Article constitute the transaction a fraudulent transfer or voidable preference. (5A Del. C. 1953, § 2-402; 55 Del. Laws, c. 349.)

RULE §2-402: Rights of Seller's Creditors Against Sold Goods:

(1) Buyer's Priority Over Seller's Creditors:

a. Rights of the Seller's Unsecured Creditors are subject to the

Buyer's rights to recover goods which have already been identified to the contract (as per §2-502 and §2-716).

b. This subsection is subject to (2) and (3) below.

(2) Seller's Fraudulent Retention of Goods:

a) The Seller's creditors may treat a sale or identification of goods as VOID if the Seller fraudulently retains possession of the goods (according to any rule of law in the state where the goods are located).

b) A Seller is not considered to be fraudulently retaining possession of goods if:

1. It is done in Good Faith; and

2. It is done in the current course of trade; and

3. The Seller is a Merchant; and

4. The goods are held for no more than a commercially reasonable time after the sale or identification of the goods.

(3) Creditor's Rights Outside Article 2 Shall Govern:

(a) Article 2 cannot reduce the rights of the Seller's creditors granted in Article 9 (Secured Transactions).

(b) Article 2 cannot reduce the Seller's creditor's rights when:

1. Goods are delivered or identified to the contract but not in the current course of trade; and

2. The Delivery or Identification is considered (according to the law of the state where the goods are located) either a:

a) Fraudulent Transfer; or

b) Voidable Preference

and 3. The goods are used either:

a) As security for a pre-existing claim for money, security, or the like; or

b) To satisfy (i.e. pay off) a pre-existing claim for money, security, or the like.

§ 2-403. Power to transfer; good faith purchase of goods; "entrusting."

(1) A purchaser of goods acquires all title which his transferor had or had power to transfer except that a purchaser of a limited interest acquires rights only to the extent of the interest purchased. A person with voidable title has power to transfer a good title to a good faith purchaser for value. When goods have been delivered under a transaction of purchase the purchaser has such power even though

(a) the transferor was deceived as to the identity of the purchaser, or

(b) the delivery was in exchange for a check which is later dishonored, or

(c) it was agreed that the transaction was to be a "cash sale", or

(d) the delivery was procured through fraud punishable as larcenous under the criminal law.

(2) Any entrusting of possession of goods to a merchant who deals in goods of that kind gives him power to transfer all rights of the entruster to a buyer in ordinary course of business.

(3) "Entrusting" includes any delivery and any acquiescence in retention of possession regardless of any condition expressed between the parties to the delivery or acquiescence and regardless of whether the procurement of the entrusting or the possessor's disposition of the goods have been such as to be larcenous under the criminal law.

(4) The rights of other purchasers of goods and of lien creditors are governed by the Articles on Secured Transactions (Article 9) and Documents of Title (Article 7). (5A Del. C. 1953, § 2-403; 55 Del. Laws, c. 349; 70 Del. Laws, c. 439, § 3.)

RULE §2-403: Good Faith Purchaser of Goods:

(1) Derivation Rule:

- ***a) <u>A Full Purchaser</u> - A purchaser of goods acquires all title which his transferor had or had the power to transfer.***
- ***b) <u>The Purchaser of Limited Interest</u> - acquires only the rights of the interest he actually purchases.***
- ***c) <u>Exception - THE GOOD FAITH PURCHASER:</u>***

1) A person with a Voidable Title has the power to transfer a good title if:

a. The transferee Purchased it in <u>Good Faith</u>

b. The Purchaser has paid <u>Value</u> (as per §1-204(44))(therefore, gifts and judicial liens are no good)

2) This exception will apply when goods have been delivered under a <u>Transaction of Purchase</u> (i.e. not theft), even if:

(a) The transferor was deceived as to the purchaser's identity; or

(b) The delivery was in exchange for a check which is later dishonored; or

(c) It was agreed that the transaction was to be a "cash sale; " or

(d) The delivery was obtained through <u>Fraud</u> (which would be punishable as larceny under the criminal law)

(2) Merchant as Bailee - A person automatically obtains the right to <u>Transfer all Rights</u> in goods (even if he doesn't own all the rights in those goods), if:

a. Someone <u>"entrusts"</u> the person with possession of the goods; and

b. The person is a <u>Merchant,</u> dealing with goods of the kind entrusted; and

c. The Merchant sells the goods to a Buyer In the Ordinary Course ("BLOC") (as per §1-201(9))

(3) "Entrusting"

a) "Entrusting" includes:

1) Any delivery; and

2) Any acquiescence in retention of possession

b) These are considered "entrusting" regardless of

1) Any agreement between the parties (for the Merchant not to sell the goods); or

2) Whether or not the "entrusting" or disposition was motivated by Fraud

(4) Rights of Other Purchasers:

a. Rights of other purchasers are governed by Articles 9 and 7. b. Article 6 also governs the rights of other purchasers.

UNIFORM COMMERCIAL CODE

ARTICLE 2 - SALES

PART 5

Performance

§ 2-501. Insurable interest in goods; manner of identification of goods.

(1) The buyer obtains a special property and an insurable interest in goods by identification of existing goods as goods to which the contract refers even though the goods so identified are non-conforming and he has an option to return or reject them. Such identification can be made at any time and in any manner explicitly agreed to by the parties. In the absence of explicit agreement identification occurs

(a) when the contract is made if it is for the sale of goods already existing and identified;

(b) if the contract is for the sale of future goods other than those described in paragraph (c), when goods are shipped, marked or otherwise designated by the seller as goods to which the contract refers;

(c) when the crops are planted or otherwise become growing crops or the young are conceived if the contract is for the sale of unborn young to be born within twelve months after contracting or for the sale of crops to be harvested within twelve months or the next normal harvest season after contracting whichever is longer.

(2) The seller retains an insurable interest in goods so long as title to or any security interest in the goods remains in him and where the identification is by the seller alone he may until default or insolvency or notification to the buyer that the identification is final substitute other goods for those identified.

(3) Nothing in this section impairs any insurable interest recognized under any other statute or rule of law. (5A Del. C. 1953, § 2-501; 55 Del. Laws, c. 349.)

RULE §2-501: Insurable Interest in Goods; Manner of Identification of Goods:

(1) Identification of Goods:

a) <u>Creation of Buyer's Interest</u> - Once <u>existing</u> goods

are identified to a contract the Buyer obtains an Insurable Interest and a Special Property Interest in the goods.

b) <u>Non-Conforming Goods</u> - The Buyer will maintain such interests in identified goods even if the goods are non-conforming; he then has the option of returning or rejecting them.

c) <u>Manner of Identification:</u>

1. <u>Agreed Mode of Identification:</u> Identification can be made at any time and in any manner explicitly agreed to by the parties.

2. <u>No Specified Mode of Identification:</u> If the parties did not explicitly agree how the goods are to be identified, identification shall occur as follows:

(a) Sale of Already Identified Existing Goods: Identification shall occur when the contract is made if the contract is for the sale of goods which are already existing and identified.

(b) Sale of Future Goods: Identification shall occur when the Seller designates specific goods as goods for the contract (ex: when they are shipped, marked or set aside for the Buyer) if the contract is for the sale of future goods (which are not crops or goods falling under (c)).

(c) Sale of Crops and Animals:

1. <u>Crops</u> - Identification shall occur when the crops are planted or become "growing crops" (if the contract is for the sale of crops to be harvested within the longer of <u>12 months</u> after or the next harvest season after the contract is made).

2. <u>Unborn Animals</u> - Identification shall occur when the young are conceived (if the contract is for the sale of unborn young to be born within <u>12 months</u> after the contract is made).

(2) Seller's Insurable Interest:

a) The Seller shall retain an <u>Insurable Interest</u> in the goods as

long as the Seller has either:
1. Title to the goods; or
2. A Security Interest in the Goods

b) <u>Substitute Goods:</u> The Seller may substitute other goods for those already identified if:
1. Identification is by the Seller alone; and
2. The Seller has not:
a. Defaulted; or
b. Become insolvent
and 3. The Seller has not yet notified the Buyer that the identification would be final.

(3) Nothing in this section impairs any insurable interest recognized under any other statute or rule of law.

§ 2-502. Buyer's right to goods on seller's repudiation, failure to deliver, or insolvency.

(1) Subject to subsections (2) and (3) and even though the goods have not been shipped, a buyer who has paid a part or all of the price of goods in which he has a special property under the provisions of the immediately preceding section may on making and keeping good a tender of any unpaid portion of their price recover them from the seller if:

(a) in the case of goods bought for personal, family, or household purposes, the seller repudiates or fails to deliver as required by the contract; or

(b) in all cases, the seller becomes insolvent within ten days after receipt of the first installment on their price.

(2) The buyer's right to recover the goods under subsection (1)(a) vests upon acquisition of a special property, even if the seller had not then repudiated or failed to deliver.

(3) If the identification creating his special property has been made by the buyer he acquires the right to recover the goods only if they conform to the contract for sale. (5A Del. C. 1953, § 2-502; 55 Del. Laws, c. 349; 72 Del. Laws, c. 401, § 9.)

RULE §2-502: Buyer's Right to Goods on Seller's Insolvency:

(1) Seller's Insolvency:

a. The Buyer may recover identified goods from the Seller if:

1. The Seller becomes insolvent within <u>10 Days</u> after the Seller received the first installment on the price of the goods

and 2. The Buyer:

a. Has made (and kept) good a tender of any unpaid portion of the price of the goods; and

b. Has paid part or all of the price of the goods; and

c. Has a Special Property Interest (as per §2-501)

b. This section shall apply even though the goods have not been shipped.

c. This section is subject to §2-502(2).

(2) Buyer Identifies Goods: If the Buyer has made the identification which creates the special property Interest he acquires the right to recover the goods <u>only if</u> the goods conform to the contract.

§ 2-503. Manner of seller's tender of delivery.

(1) Tender of delivery requires that the seller put and hold conforming goods at the buyer's disposition and give the buyer any notification reasonably necessary to enable him to take delivery. The manner, time and place for tender are determined by the agreement and this Article, and in particular

(a) tender must be at a reasonable hour, and if it is of goods they must be kept available for the period reasonably necessary to enable the buyer to take possession; but

(b) unless otherwise agreed the buyer must furnish facilities reasonably suited to the receipt of the goods.

(2) Where the case is within the next section respecting shipment tender requires that the seller comply with its provisions.

(3) Where the seller is required to deliver at a particular destination tender requires that he comply with subsection (1) and also in any appropriate case tender documents as described in subsections (4) and (5) of this section.

(4) Where goods are in the possession of a bailee and are to be delivered without being moved

(a) tender requires that the seller either tender a negotiable document of title covering such goods or procure acknowledgment by the bailee of the buyer's right to possession of the goods; but

(b) tender to the buyer of a non-negotiable document of title or of a written direction to the bailee to deliver is sufficient tender unless the buyer seasonably objects, and receipt by the bailee of notification of the buyer's rights fixes those rights as against the bailee and all third persons; but risk of loss of the goods and of any failure by the bailee to honor the non-negotiable document of title or to obey the direction remains on the seller until the buyer has had a reasonable time to present the document or direction, and a refusal by the bailee to honor the document or to obey the direction defeats the tender.

(5) Where the contract requires the seller to deliver documents

(a) he must tender all such documents in correct form, except as provided in this Article with respect to bills of lading in a set (subsection (2) of Section 2-323); and

(b) tender through customary banking channels is sufficient and dishonor of a draft accompanying the documents constitutes non-acceptance or rejection. (5A Del. C. 1953, § 2-503; 55 Del. Laws, c. 349.)

RULE §2-503: Manner of Seller's Tender of Delivery:

(1) Tender of Delivery:

i) <u>Requirements for Tender:</u>

a) The Seller must <u>Put and Hold</u> conforming goods at the Buyer's disposition.

and b) The Seller must give the Buyer any type of <u>notification</u> reasonably necessary to enable the Buyer to take delivery.

and ii) <u>Manner, Place & Time of Tender:</u>

Manner, time and place are determined by the agreement and Article 2, and specifically the following:

(a) Time for Tender of Delivery:

1. Tender must be at a reasonable hour.

2. If Goods - they must be kept available for a sufficient period reasonably necessary for Buyer to take possession.

(b) Place to Deliver: The Buyer must furnish a facility reasonably suited to receive the goods (unless otherwise agreed).

(2) Shipment by Seller: Where shipment is by Seller (as per §2-504), the Seller must tender according to the provisions of §2-504.

(3) Delivery at a Particular Destination: If Seller is required to deliver goods to a particular destination, the Seller must:
a) Comply with §2-503(1)
and b) Tender documents as per §2-503(4) and (5) (where appropriate)

(4) Goods In A Bailee's Possession To Be Delivered Without Being Moved:

(a) Tendering a Negotiable Document of Title - Seller must either:

1) Tender a Negotiable Document of Title (covering the goods); or

2) Have the Bailee acknowledge the Buyer's right to possession of the goods

(b) Tendering a Non-Negotiable Document of Title (or written direction to the Bailee to deliver):

1) A Non-Negotiable DOT or a Written Direction to the Bailee is sufficient to tender delivery unless the Buyer seasonably objects.

2) Once the Bailee is notified of the Buyer's rights, the Buyer's rights will be fixed against the Bailee and all third persons.

3) The Seller bears the risk of: a)
Loss; and
b) Failure of Bailee to honor the non-negotiable document of title; and

c) Failure of Bailee to obey a written direction

4) The Seller's risk remains until the Buyer has had a reasonable time to present the document or written direction.

5) Tender is defeated by the Bailee's refusal to honor the instrument/written direction.

(5) Contracts Requiring Seller to Deliver Documents:

(a) <u>Requirements of Documents:</u>

1. The Seller must tender each required document.

2. The documents must be:

a) The actual documents required by the contract; and

b) In their correct form

3. <u>Exception:</u> This section shall not apply to Bills of Lading in a set (see §2-323).

(b) <u>Tendering with Banks:</u>

1. Tender through customary banking channels is sufficient.

2. If an accompanying draft is dishonored, the goods are deemed to be either:

a. Rejected or

b. Not accepted

§ 2-504. Shipment by seller.

Where the seller is required or authorized to send the goods to the buyer and the contract does not require him to deliver them at a particular destination, then unless otherwise agreed he must

(a) put the goods in the possession of such a carrier and make such a contract for their transportation as may be reasonable having regard to the nature of the goods and other circumstances of the case; and

(b) obtain and promptly deliver or tender in due form any document necessary to enable the buyer to obtain possession of the goods or otherwise required by the agreement or by usage of trade; and

(c) promptly notify the buyer of the shipment.

Failure to notify the buyer under paragraph (c) or to make a proper contract under paragraph (a) is a ground for rejection only if material delay or loss ensues. (5A Del. C. 1953, § 2-504; 55 Del. Laws, c. 349.)

RULE §2-504: Shipment by Seller:

1. This Section applies only if:

a. The Seller is required or authorized to send the goods to the Buyer; and

b. The contract doesn't require the Seller to deliver the goods to a particular destination and c. The parties have not otherwise agreed

2. The Seller must (unless otherwise agreed):

(a) <u>Arrange for Goods to be Shipped:</u>

1. Put the goods in the Carrier's possession; and

2. Make a contract for the transportation of the goods in a manner reasonable under the circumstances (considering the type of goods to be shipped (ex: frozen food, fragile glass)).

and (b) <u>Send Documents:</u> Obtain and promptly deliver or tender any documents (in due form) which:

i) Buyer may need to obtain possession of the goods (ex: BOL); or

ii) Are otherwise required by the agreement; or

iii) Are otherwise required by Usage of Trade and

(c) <u>Promptly notify the Buyer of shipment</u>

3. The following are grounds for Rejection only if <u>material delay</u> or loss results:

a) Failure to make a proper shipping contract (as per §2-504(a)) or

b) Failure to promptly notify Buyer of the shipment (as per §2-504(c))

§ 2-505. Seller's shipment under reservation.

(1) Where the seller has identified goods to the contract by or before shipment:

(a) his procurement of a negotiable bill of lading to his own order or otherwise reserves in him a security interest in the goods. His procurement of the bill to the order of a financing agency or of the buyer indicates in addition only the seller's expectation of transferring that interest to the person named.

(b) a non-negotiable bill of lading to himself or his nominee reserves possession of the goods as security but except in a case of conditional delivery (subsection (2) of Section 2-507) a non-negotiable bill of lading naming the buyer as consignee reserves no security interest even though the seller retains possession of the bill of lading.

(2) When shipment by the seller with reservation of a security interest is in violation of the contract for sale it constitutes an improper contract for transportation within the preceding section but impairs neither the rights given to the buyer by shipment and identification of the goods to the contract nor the seller's power as a holder of a negotiable document. (5A Del. C. 1953, § 2-505; 55 Del. Laws, c. 349.)

RULE §2-505: Seller's Shipment Under Reservation:

(1) Goods Identified By Seller By or Before Shipment:

- ***(a) <u>Negotiable BOL:</u> If the Seller has identified goods to a contract by or before shipment, then:***
  1. ***The Seller may reserve a Security Interest in the goods by preparing a Negotiable Bill of Lading to his order (or otherwise); and***
  2. ***Making the Negotiable BOL to the order of the <u>Buyer</u> or a <u>Financing Agency</u> will not impair the reservation of the security interest (it only indicates the Seller's expectations of transferability of interest).***
- ***(b) <u>Non-Negotiable BOL:</u> If the Seller has identified goods to a contract by or before delivery, then:***
  1. ***<u>Unconditional Delivery:</u> A non-negotiable BOL naming the Seller or his nominee reserves possession of the goods as a security.***

2. <u>Conditional Delivery</u> (as per §2-507(2)): The Seller will not reserve himself a Security Interest if he uses a non-negotiable BOL which names the Buyer as the Consignee (even if the Seller retains possession of the BOL).

(2) Seller's Reservation In Violation of Contract: If the Seller's reservation of a Security Interest violates the contract of sale:

a) The contract is considered an improper contract for transportation (as per §2-504); but

b) The effectiveness of the contract is not impaired regarding:

1. The rights given to the Buyer by the shipment and identification of the goods to the contract; and

2. The Seller's powers as a Holder of a Negotiable Document

§ 2-506. Rights of financing agency.

(1) A financing agency by paying or purchasing for value a draft which relates to a shipment of goods acquires to the extent of the payment or purchase and in addition to its own rights under the draft and any document of title securing it any rights of the shipper in the goods including the right to stop delivery and the shipper's right to have the draft honored by the buyer.

(2) The right to reimbursement of a financing agency which has in good faith honored or purchased the draft under commitment to or authority from the buyer is not impaired by subsequent discovery of defects with reference to any relevant document which was apparently regular on its face. (5A Del. C. 1953, § 2-506; 55 Del. Laws, c. 349.)

RULE §2-506: Rights of Financing Agency:

(1) Financing Agency's Rights From Purchase of Documentary Draft:

a. A Financing Agency may obtain a shipper's rights in the

goods by paying or purchasing (for value) a Draft relating to the shipment of the goods (ex: a draft made against an invoice, a draft made against a delivery order).

b. The rights the Financing Agency will obtain from the shipper include:

1) The right to stop delivery

2) The Shipper's right to have the draft honored by the Buyer

c. The Financing Agency must pay <u>value</u> (as per §1-201(44)) for the draft.

d. The Financing Agency may only acquire the shipper's right to the extent of the payment or purchase of the draft.

e. These rights are in addition to the Financing Agency's own rights under the draft and any documents of title securing them.

(2) Rights of Reimbursement: A Financing Agency's rights in a draft will not be impaired by any defects in relevant documents if:

a. The documents looked regular on their face; and

b. The defects were not discovered until after the Financing Agency purchased or honored the draft; and

c. The Financing Agency either:

1) <u>Honored</u> the Draft in Good Faith; or

2) <u>Purchased</u> the Draft under a commitment to the Buyer; or

3) <u>Purchased</u> the Draft under the authority of the Buyer

§ 2-507. Effect of seller's tender; delivery on condition.

(1) Tender of delivery is a condition to the buyer's duty to accept the goods and, unless otherwise agreed, to his duty to pay for them. Tender entitles the seller to acceptance of the goods and to payment according to the contract.

(2) Where payment is due and demanded on the delivery to the buyer of goods or documents of title, his right as against the seller to retain or dispose of them is conditional upon his making the payment due. (5A Del. C. 1953, § 2-507; 55 Del. Laws, c. 349.)

RULE §2-507: Effect of Seller's Tender; Delivery on Condition:

(1) Effect of Tender:

- ***a. <u>Buyer's Obligation:</u> Tender of delivery is a condition to the Buyer's obligation to:***
    - ***1. Accept the goods; and***
    - ***2. Pay for the goods (unless otherwise agreed)***

- ***b. <u>Seller's Entitlement:</u> Tender entitles the Seller to:***
    - ***1. The Buyer's acceptance of the goods; and***
    - ***2. Payment (according to the contract)***

(2) Conditional Delivery:

The Buyer's rights to retain or dispose of the goods is conditional upon making payment due to the Seller, if:

- ***a. <u>Payment is due</u> upon delivery (of goods or documents of title) to the Buyer; and***
- ***b. <u>Seller demanded payment</u> upon delivery (of goods or documents of title) to the Buyer***

§ 2-508. Cure by seller of improper tender or delivery; replacement.

(1) Where any tender or delivery by the seller is rejected because non-conforming and the time for performance has not yet expired, the seller may seasonably notify the buyer of his intention to cure and may then within the contract time make a conforming delivery.

(2) Where the buyer rejects a non-conforming tender which the seller had reasonable grounds to believe would be acceptable with or without money allowance the seller may if he seasonably notifies the buyer have a further reasonable time to substitute a conforming tender. (5A Del. C. 1953, § 2-508; 55 Del. Laws, c. 349.)

RULE §2-508: Cure By Seller for Improper Tender or Delivery; Replacement:

(1) Non-Conforming Goods: The Seller may seasonably notify the Buyer of his intention to cure, and may then ship conforming goods if:
- ***a) Goods are rejected because they are non-conforming***
- ***b) The time for performance has not expired***
- ***c) The Seller re-ships conforming goods before the expiration of performance (i.e. before the delivery date)***

(2) Goods Seller Deemed Conforming: Seller may extend time of delivery and ship conforming goods if:
- ***a) The goods are rejected because they are non-conforming; and***
- ***b) The Seller had reasonable grounds to believe they would be acceptable (with or without a money allowance); and***
- ***c) Seller seasonably notifies the Buyer and b) The extension is reasonable***

§ 2-509. Risk of loss in the absence of breach.

(1) Where the contract requires or authorizes the seller to ship the goods by carrier

(a) if it does not require him to deliver them at a particular destination, the risk of loss passes to the buyer when the goods are duly delivered to the carrier even though the shipment is under reservation (Section 2-505); but

(b) if it does require him to deliver them at a particular destination and the goods are there duly tendered while in the possession of the carrier, the risk of loss passes to the buyer when the goods are there duly so tendered as to enable the buyer to take delivery.

(2) Where the goods are held by a bailee to be delivered without being moved, the risk of loss passes to the buyer

(a) on his receipt of a negotiable document of title covering the goods; or

(b) on acknowledgment by the bailee of the buyer's right to possession of the goods; or

(c) after his receipt of a non-negotiable document of title or other written direction to deliver, as provided in subsection (4)(b) of Section 2-503.

(3) In any case not within subsection (1) or (2), the risk of loss passes to the buyer on his receipt of the goods if the seller is a merchant; otherwise the risk passes to the buyer on tender of delivery.

(4) The provisions of this section are subject to contrary agreement of the parties and to the provisions of this Article on sale on approval (Section 2-327) and on effect of breach on risk of loss (Section 2-510). (5A Del. C. 1953, § 2-509; 55 Del. Laws, c. 349.)

RULE §2-509: Risk of Loss in the Absence of Breach:

(1) Contracts Requiring or Authorizing Seller to Ship the Goods by the Carrier (FOB Carrier):

- ***(a) Shipment Contract: The Risk of Loss passes to the Buyer when the goods are duly delivered to the Carrier, if the contract does not require the Seller to deliver the goods to a particular destination (even if the shipment is under "Reservation" (as per §2-505))***
- ***(b) Destination Contract: The Risk of Loss passes to the Buyer when the goods are so tendered to enable the Buyer to take delivery if:***
  1. ***The contract does not require the Seller to deliver the goods .to a particular destination; and***
  2. ***The goods are tendered while in the possession of a Carrier***

(2) When Goods are held by a Bailee to be Delivered without Being Moved - Risk of Loss passes to the Buyer when:

- ***(a) He received a <u>Negotiable Document of Title</u> covering the goods; or***
- ***(b) The Bailee acknowledges the Buyer's right to possess***

the goods; or

(c) He received a <u>Non-Negotiable Document of Title</u> (or other written direction to deliver (as per §2-503(4)(b))

(3) <u>All other cases</u> - Risk passes to Buyer:

(a) When he receives the goods - if Seller is a Merchant

(b) Upon Tender of Delivery - if Seller is not a Merchant

(4) This section is subject to:

(a) Agreements of the parties

(b) §2-327 (Sale on Approval)

(c) §2-510 (Effect of Breach on Risk of Loss)

§ 2-510. Effect of breach on risk of loss.

(1) Where a tender or delivery of goods so fails to conform to the contract as to give a right of rejection the risk of their loss remains on the seller until cure or acceptance.

(2) Where the buyer rightfully revokes acceptance he may to the extent of any deficiency in his effective insurance coverage treat the risk of loss as having rested on the seller from the beginning.

(3) Where the buyer as to conforming goods already identified to the contract for sale repudiates or is otherwise in breach before risk of their loss has passed to him, the seller may to the extent of any deficiency in his effective insurance coverage treat the risk of loss as resting on the buyer for a commercially reasonable time. (5A Del. C. 1953, § 2-510; 55 Del. Laws, c. 349.)

RULE §2-510: Risk of Loss with Breach:

(1) Seller's Breach:

Risk of loss remains on the <u>Seller</u> until Cure or Acceptance if: a) Tender or Delivery fails to conform to the contract and b) The non-conformity gives rise to a Right of Rejection

(2) Buyer's Revocation of Acceptance:

The Buyer may treat the risk of loss as the Seller's from the

beginning of the contract (as if risk of loss never passes to the Buyer)

a) If the Buyer rightfully revokes acceptance; and

b) To the extent the Buyer's insurance is deficient

(3) Buyer's Breach:

The Seller may treat the risk of loss as the <u>Buyer's</u> (To the extent the Seller's insurance was deficient) for a commercially reasonable time if:

a) The goods were already identified to the contract and

b) The goods conformed to the contract and

c) The Buyer Repudiates/Breaches before risk of loss passes to him

§ 2-511. Tender of payment by buyer; payment by check.

(1) Unless otherwise agreed tender of payment is a condition to the seller's duty to tender and complete any delivery.

(2) Tender of payment is sufficient when made by any means or in any manner current in the ordinary course of business unless the seller demands payment in legal tender and gives any extension of time reasonably necessary to procure it.

(3) Subject to the provisions of this subtitle on the effect of an instrument on an obligation (Section 3-802), payment by check is conditional and is defeated as between the parties by dishonor of the check on due presentment. (5A Del. C. 1953, § 2-511; 55 Del. Laws, c. 349.)

RULE §2-511: Tender of Payment:

(1) Tender of Payment is a condition to the Seller's duty to tender and complete any delivery (unless otherwise agreed).

(2) Tender of Payment is sufficient if it is made by any manner in the ordinary course of business, unless:

a) Seller demands money (legal tender); and
b) Seller gives an extension of time reasonably necessary for Buyer to comply

(3) Payment by check is conditional and is defeated if it is dishonored on due presentment (Subject to §3-802 (Effect of an Instrument on an Obligation)).

§ 2-512. Payment by buyer before inspection.

(1) Where the contract requires payment before inspection non-conformity of the goods does not excuse the buyer from so making payment unless

(a) the non-conformity appears without inspection; or

(b) despite tender of the required documents the circumstances would justify injunction against honor under this subtitle (Section 5-109(b)).

(2) Payment pursuant to subsection (1) does not constitute an acceptance of goods or impair the buyer's right to inspect or any of his remedies. (5A Del. C. 1953, § 2-512; 55 Del. Laws, c. 349; 71 Del. Laws, c. 393, § 3.)

RULE §2-512: Payment by Buyer Before Inspection:

(1) Payment Required Before Inspection: If a contract requires goods to be paid for before inspection (ex: Seller will tender documents), a non-conformity of the goods will not be an excuse for non-payment, unless:
(a) The non-conformity appears without inspection (i.e. when the goods are delivered, the non-conformities are very obvious); or
(b) The circumstances would justify an injunction against honoring the Seller's tender of the required documents (as per §5-114)

(2) Effects of Payment Before Inspection:
(a) PAYMENT (as per §2-512(1)) DOES NOT

CONSTITUTE ACCEPTANCE.

(b) Payment does not impair the Buyer's right to inspect the goods (before accepting them).

(c) Payment does not impair any of the Buyer's remedies.

§ 2-513. Buyer's right to inspection of goods.

(1) Unless otherwise agreed and subject to subsection (3), where goods are tendered or delivered or identified to the contract for sale, the buyer has a right before payment or acceptance to inspect them at any reasonable place and time and in any reasonable manner. When the seller is required or authorized to send the goods to the buyer, the inspection may be after their arrival.

(2) Expenses of inspection must be borne by the buyer but may be recovered from the seller if the goods do not conform and are rejected.

(3) Unless otherwise agreed and subject to the provisions of this Article on C.I.F. contracts (subsection (3) of Section 2-321), the buyer is not entitled to inspect the goods before payment of the price when the contract provides

(a) for delivery "C.O.D." or on other like terms; or

(b) for payment against documents of title, except where such payment is due only after the goods are to become available for inspection.

(4) A place or method of inspection fixed by the parties is presumed to be exclusive but unless otherwise expressly agreed it does not postpone identification or shift the place for delivery or for passing the risk of loss. If compliance becomes impossible, inspection shall be as provided in this section unless the place or method fixed was clearly intended as an indispensable condition failure of which avoids the contract. (5A Del. C. 1953, § 2-513; 55 Del. Laws, c. 349.)

RULE §2-513: Buyer's Right to Inspect Goods:

(1) Buyer's Right to Inspection of Goods:

- ***a) The Buyer has a right to inspect the goods before payment or acceptance if the goods are:***
  - ***1. Tendered; or***
  - ***2. Delivered; or***
  - ***3. Identified to the contract for sale***
- ***b) The Buyer has a right to inspect the goods:***
  - ***1. At any reasonable place and time; and***
  - ***2. In any reasonable manner***
- ***c) When the Seller is required or authorized to send the goods to the Buyer, the inspection may be after their arrival.***
- ***d) This subsection may be changed by agreement of the parties, and is subject to §2-513(3).***

(2) <u>Expense of Inspection:</u>

- ***a) Expenses must be borne by the Buyer.***
- ***b) If the goods do not conform and are rejected, the Buyer may recover inspection expenses from Seller.***

(3) No Right to Inspect:

- ***(a) The Buyer is not entitled to inspect the goods before payment if the contract provides:***
  - ***(i) For delivery "C. O. D. " (or on other similar terms); or***
  - ***(ii) For payment against DOT's (except where such payment is due only after the goods are to become available for inspection)***
- ***(b) This subsection may be changed by agreement of parties, and is subject to §2-321(3) (dealing with C.I.F. contracts).***

(4) Fixed Place/Method of Inspection:

- ***(a) A place or method of inspection fixed by the parties is presumed to be exclusive.***
- ***(b) Unless otherwise agreed, such an agreement***

does not:

1. Postpone identification; or

2. Change the place for delivery; or

3. Shift the passing of risk of loss

(c) <u>If compliance with fixed terms becomes impossible</u> -

Buyer shall have a right to inspect (as per §2-513), unless the fixed place/method was clearly intended as an indispensable condition, failure of which avoids the contract.

§ 2-514. When documents deliverable on acceptance; when on payment.

Unless otherwise agreed documents against which a draft is drawn are to be delivered to the drawee on acceptance of the draft if it is payable more than three days after presentment; otherwise, only on payment. (5A Del. C. 1953, § 2-514; 55 Del. Laws, c. 349.)

RULE §2-514: When Documents Deliverable on Acceptance; When on Payment:

1) <u>Documents Delivered Upon Acceptance</u> - Documents (against which a draft is drawn) are to be delivered to the <u>Drawee</u> upon Acceptance of the draft if:

a) The Draft is payable more than <u>3 Days</u> after presentment; and

b) The Parties do not otherwise agree

2) <u>Documents Delivered Upon Payment</u> - Documents (against which a draft is drawn) are to be delivered to the <u>Drawee</u> upon Payment of the draft if:

a) The Draft is not payable more than <u>3 Days</u> after presentment; and

b) The Parties agree

§ 2-515. Preserving evidence of goods in dispute.

In furtherance of the adjustment of any claim or dispute

(a) either party on reasonable notification to the other and for the purpose of ascertaining the facts and preserving evidence has the right to inspect, test and sample the goods including such of them as may be in the possession or control of the other; and

(b) the parties may agree to a third party inspection or survey to determine the conformity or condition of the goods and may agree that the findings shall be binding upon them in any subsequent litigation or adjustment. (5A Del. C. 1953, § 2-515; 55 Del. Laws, c. 349.)

RULE §2-515: Preserving Evidence of Goods in Dispute:

(a) Right To Inspect, Test or Sample:

Either party has the right to Inspect, Test and Sample the goods (including those that are possession or control of the other party), if:

1. ***Notice: The party reasonably notifies the other party that he intends to inspect, test or sample the goods; and***
2. ***Purpose of Inspection: The inspection, sampling or testing is for the purpose of ascertaining the facts and preserving evidence; and***
3. ***Inspection is "in furtherance of the adjustment of any claim or dispute."***

(b) Third Party Inspections:

1. ***The parties may agree to have a Third Party Inspection or Survey of the goods to determine:***
   a) If the goods conform to the contract
   b) The condition of the goods

2. ***The parties may agree that all findings by the Third Party shall be binding upon them in any subsequent litigation or adjustment***

UNIFORM COMMERCIAL CODE

ARTICLE 2 - SALES

PART 6

Breach, Repudiation and Excuse

§ 2-601. Buyer's rights on improper delivery.

Subject to the provisions of this Article on breach in installment contracts (Section 2-612) and unless otherwise agreed under the sections on contractual limitations of remedy (Sections 2-718 and 2-719), if the goods or the tender of delivery fail in any respect to conform to the contract, the buyer may

(a) reject the whole; or

(b) accept the whole; or

(c) accept any commercial unit or units and reject the rest. (5A Del. C. 1953, § 2-601; 55 Del. Laws, c. 349.)

RULE §2-601: Buyer's Rights on Improper Delivery:

1. Remedies For Imperfect Tender: If the goods or the tender of delivery <u>in any way</u> fail to conform to the contract, then Buyer may:
- ***(a) Reject the whole shipment; or***
- ***(b) Accept the whole shipment; or***
- ***(c) Accept any "commercial unit," and reject the rest***

2. This rule is subject to
- ***(a) §2-612 (Breach of Installment Contracts)***
- ***(b) Liquidated Remedy Agreements (under §2-718 and §2-719)***

§ 2-602. Manner and effect of rightful rejection.

(1) Rejection of goods must be within a reasonable time after their delivery or tender. It is ineffective unless the buyer seasonably notifies the seller.

(2) Subject to the provisions of the two following sections on rejected goods (Sections 2-603 and 2-604),

(a) after rejection any exercise of ownership by the buyer with respect to any commercial unit is wrongful as against the seller; and

(b) if the buyer has before rejection taken physical possession of goods in which he does not have a security interest under the provisions of this Article (subsection (3) of Section 2-711), he is under a duty after rejection to hold them with reasonable care at the seller's disposition for a time sufficient to permit the seller to remove them; but

(c) the buyer has no further obligations with regard to goods rightfully rejected.

(3) The seller's rights with respect to goods wrongfully rejected are governed by the provisions of this Article on Seller's remedies in general (Section 2-703). (5A Del. C. 1953, § 2-602; 55 Del. Laws, c. 349.)

RULE §2-602: Manner and Effect of Rightful Rejection:

(1) When to Reject:

- ***(a) The Buyer must seasonably notify the Seller that it is rejecting the goods.***
- ***(b) Rejection will be ineffective if it is not made within a reasonable time after delivery or tender occurs.***

(2) Buyer's Rights and Obligations (subject to §2-603 and §2-604):

- ***(a) After rejection, any "exercise of ownership" over the goods (by the Buyer) is considered wrongful against the Seller; and***
- ***(b) The Buyer will have an obligation to hold the goods with reasonable care for a reasonable time after rejection (in order to allow the Seller to remove them) <u>if:</u>***
    - ***1. The Buyer has taken physical possession of the***

goods before he rejected them; and

2. The Buyer does not have a Security Interest in the goods (as per §2-711(3))

and (c) The Buyer has no further obligations with regard to rightfully rejected goods (unless he is a Merchant, in which case §2-603 applies).

(3) Seller's Rights: The Seller's rights in wrongfully rejected goods are governed by §2-703 (Seller's Remedies).

§ 2-603. Merchant buyer's duties as to rightfully rejected goods.

(1) Subject to any security interest in the buyer (subsection (3) of Section 2-711), when the seller has no agent or place of business at the market of rejection a merchant buyer is under a duty after rejection of goods in his possession or control to follow any reasonable instructions received from the seller with respect to the goods and in the absence of such instructions to make reasonable efforts to sell them for the seller's account if they are perishable or threaten to decline in value speedily. Instructions are not reasonable if on demand indemnity for expenses is not forthcoming.

(2) When the buyer sells goods under subsection (1), he is entitled to reimbursement from the seller or out of the proceeds for reasonable expenses of caring for and selling them, and if the expenses include no selling commission then to such commission as is usual in the trade or if there is none to a reasonable sum not exceeding ten per cent on the gross proceeds.

(3) In complying with this section the buyer is held only to good faith and good faith conduct hereunder is neither acceptance nor conversion nor the basis of an action for damages. (5A Del. C. 1953, § 2-603; 55 Del. Laws, c. 349.)

RULE §2-603: Merchant Buyer's Rightful Rejection:

(1) Buyer's Duties Upon Rejection:

a) After rejection, any <u>Merchant</u> Buyer must follow any reasonable instruction received from the Seller, with respect to such goods if:

1. If Seller has no agent or place of business where goods are rejected; and

2. After rejection goods are still in the Buyer's possession or control

b) Upon rejection, the Buyer must make reasonable efforts to sell the goods for the Seller if:

1. The Seller has no agent or place of business where goods are rejected; and

2. After rejection goods are still in the Buyer's possession or control; and

3. The Seller left no other reasonable instructions; and

4. The goods are perishable or threaten to speedily decline in value

c) Instructions are not reasonable if, on the Buyer's demand, indemnity for expenses is not forthcoming.

d) This subsection is subject to any S/I in the Buyer (as per §2-711(3)).

(2) Reimbursement to Buyer: When the Buyer sells goods under §2-603(1), he is entitled to <u>reimbursement</u> from the Seller (or out of the proceeds of the sale) for:

a. Reasonable selling expenses

b. Reasonable expenses incurred in caring for the goods

c. Selling Commissions, if they are:

1. Not included in expenses; and

2. <u>Either:</u>

a) Reasonable in the trade/industry; or

b) A Reasonable Sum (if no industry norm), not to exceed 10% of gross proceeds.

(3) Buyer's Standard of Good Faith:

a) The Buyer is held to a standard of Good Faith.

b) Good Faith conduct will not be considered Acceptance, Conversion, or a basis of an action for damages.

§ 2-604. Buyer's options as to salvage of rightfully rejected goods.

Subject to the provisions of the immediately preceding section on perishables, if the seller gives no instructions within a reasonable time after notification of rejection the buyer may store the rejected goods for the seller's account or reship them to him or resell them for the seller's account with reimbursement as provided in the preceding section.

Such action is not acceptance or conversion. (5A Del. C. 1953, § 2-604; 55 Del. Laws, c. 349.)

RULE §2-604: Buyer's Option to Salvage Rightfully Rejected Goods:

1. ***Buyer's Options: The Buyer has the following options with respect to rightfully rejected goods:***
    a. ***Store the rejected goods for the seller***
    b. ***Reship the goods back to the seller***
    c. ***Resell the goods on behalf of the seller and reimburse him***

2. ***The Buyer may only exercise these options if the seller does not give the Buyer instructions within a reasonable time after notification of rejection.***

3. ***This section is subject to §2-603 (duty to resell) if:***
    a. ***The Buyer is a Merchant; and***
    b. ***The goods are perishable***

4. ***These actions will not be considered Acceptance or Conversion.***

§ 2-605. Waiver of buyer's objections by failure to particularize.

(1) The buyer's failure to state in connection with rejection a particular defect which is ascertainable by reasonable inspection precludes him from relying on the unstated defect to justify rejection or to establish breach

(a) where the seller could have cured it if stated seasonably; or

(b) between merchants when the seller has after rejection made a request in writing for a full and final written statement of all defects on which the buyer proposes to rely.

(2) Payment against documents made without reservation of rights precludes recovery of the payment for defects apparent on the face of the documents. (5A Del. C. 1953, § 2-605; 55 Del. Laws, c. 349.)

RULE §2-605: Waiver of Buyer's Right to Reject:

(1) If Buyer does not give specific reasons for rejecting goods, he waives the right to reject them (based on that defect) if:
- ***i) The defects are ascertainable by reasonable inspection and***
- ***ii) Either:***
  - ***(a) The Seller could have fixed the problem seasonably (if the reason was stated); or***
  - ***(b) Between Merchants - the Merchant Seller has requested a written statement of defects from the Merchant Buyer***

(2) Payment Against Documents: Recovery of payments for defects apparent on the face of documents will be precluded if payment is made:
- ***(a) Against the documents; and***
- ***(b) "Without reservation"***

§ 2-606. What constitutes acceptance of goods.

(1) Acceptance of goods occurs when the buyer

(a) after a reasonable opportunity to inspect the goods signifies to the seller that the goods are conforming or that he will take or retain them in spite of their non-conformity; or

(b) fails to make an effective rejection (subsection (1) of Section 2-602), but such acceptance does not occur until the buyer has had a reasonable opportunity to inspect them; or

(c) does any act inconsistent with the seller's ownership; but if such act is wrongful as against the seller it is an acceptance only if ratified by him.

(2) Acceptance of a part of any commercial unit is acceptance of that entire unit. (5A Del. C. 1953, § 2-606; 55 Del. Laws, c. 349.)

RULE §2-606: Acceptance Of Goods:

(1) Acceptance of Goods occurs when Buyer:

(a) Signifies to Seller (after reasonable opportunity to inspect them) that either:

1. The goods conform to the contract; or

2. The Buyer will take or retain the goods even though there is a non-conformity

or (b) Fails to make an effective rejection (as per §2-602(1)) after a reasonable opportunity to inspect

or (c) Does any act inconsistent with Seller's ownership (i.e. if such an act is wrongful, acceptance is only at the Seller's option)

(2) Acceptance of part of a "commercial unit" is considered acceptance of the whole unit.

§ 2-607. Effect of acceptance; notice of breach; burden of establishing breach after acceptance; notice of claim or litigation to person answerable over.

(1) The buyer must pay at the contract rate for any goods accepted.

(2) Acceptance of goods by the buyer precludes rejection of the goods accepted and if made with knowledge of a non-conformity cannot be revoked because of it unless the acceptance was on the reasonable assumption that the non-conformity would be seasonably cured but acceptance does not of itself impair any other remedy provided by this Article for non-conformity.

(3) Where a tender has been accepted

(a) the buyer must within a reasonable time after he discovers or should have discovered any breach notify the seller of breach or be barred from any remedy; and

(b) if the claim is one for infringement or the like (subsection (3) of Section 2-312) and the buyer is sued as a result of such a breach he must so notify the seller within a reasonable time after he receives notice of the litigation or be barred from any remedy over for liability established by the litigation.

(4) The burden is on the buyer to establish any breach with respect to the goods accepted.

(5) Where the buyer is sued for breach of a warranty or other obligation for which his seller is answerable over

(a) he may give his seller written notice of the litigation. If the notice states that the seller may come in and defend and that if the seller does not do so he will be bound in any action against him by his buyer by any determination of fact common to the two litigations, then unless the seller after seasonable receipt of the notice does come in and defend he is so bound.

(b) if the claim is one for infringement or the like (subsection (3) of Section 2-312) the original seller may demand in writing that his buyer turn over to him control of the litigation including settlement or else be barred from any remedy over and if he also agrees to bear all expense and to satisfy any adverse judgment, then unless the buyer after seasonable receipt of the demand does turn over control the buyer is so barred.

(6) The provisions of subsections (3), (4) and (5) apply to any obligation of a buyer to hold the seller harmless against infringement or the like (subsection (3) of Section 2-312). (5A Del. C. 1953, § 2-607; 55 Del. Laws, c. 349.)

RULE §2-607: Effect of Acceptance:

(1) Price of Accepted Goods: The Buyer must pay the contract price (i.e. the price of the goods as stated in the contract) for any goods accepted.

(2) Rejection and Revocation:

- ***a. Goods cannot be rejected after they have been accepted.***
- ***b. Goods cannot be <u>revoked</u> due to a non-conformity if they were accepted with knowledge of the non-conformity <u>unless</u> the Buyer reasonably assumed that the Seller would fix the non-conformity.***
- ***c. Acceptance itself does not impair other Article 2 remedies for non-conforming goods.***

(3) Acceptance of Tender: If tender has been accepted:

(a) <u>Breach:</u>

1. The Buyer must notify the Seller of any breach within a reasonable time after discovering such a breach (or a reasonable time after he should have discovered it).

2. If the Buyer does not notify the Seller of such breach within a reasonable time, the Buyer will be barred from any remedy.

(b) <u>Infringement:</u>

1. The Buyer must notify the Seller of any litigation against the Buyer if:

a) The Buyer is sued as a result of the Seller's breach; and

b) The claim is for infringement (or the like (as per §2-312(3))

2. If the Buyer does not send the Seller such notice within a reasonable time after the Buyer learns of the litigation, the Buyer will not be able to use any remedies against the Seller to recover the liability damages arising out of the litigation.

(4) Burden of Proof: The <u>Buyer</u> has the burden of proving a breach with respect to the accepted goods.

(5) When Buyer is Sued for Seller's Wrong: When the Buyer is sued for an obligation (ex: breach of warranty) which his Seller may be responsible for:

(a) The facts determined in the suit against the Buyer will be binding in any similar suit which the Buyer may start against the Seller if:

1) The Seller is answerable to the Buyer for the breach of obligation; and

2) The Buyer sent the Seller a <u>written</u> notice of the litigation; and

3) The notice gave the Seller an opportunity to defend himself in the case and described the consequences of not appearing; and

4) The Seller neglected to defend himself within a reasonable time after he received the notice

(b) <u>Infringement:</u>

1) The original Seller may demand that his Buyer give him control of the litigation (including settlement).

2) The Buyer will not be able to use any remedies against the Seller to recover the liability damages arising out of the litigation if:

a. The claim was one of infringement (or the like (as per §2-312(3)); and

b. The original Seller demanded control of the litigation; and

c. The Seller's demand was in <u>writing;</u> and

d. The Seller agreed to pay for:

1. All litigation expenses; and

2. Any adverse judgment; and

e. The Buyer does not turn the case over to the Seller within a reasonable time after receiving the Seller's demand.

(6) Applicability: Subsections (3), (4) and (5) (above) apply to any obligation of a Buyer to hold the Seller harmless against infringement (or the like (as per §2-312(3))).

§ 2-608. Revocation of acceptance in whole or in part.

(1) The buyer may revoke his acceptance of a lot or commercial unit whose non-conformity substantially impairs its value to him if he has accepted it

(a) on the reasonable assumption that its non-conformity would be cured and it has not been seasonably cured; or

(b) without discovery of such non-conformity if his acceptance was reasonably induced either by the difficulty of discovery before acceptance or by the seller's assurances.

(2) Revocation of acceptance must occur within a reasonable time after the buyer discovers or should have discovered the ground for it and before any substantial change in condition of the goods which is not caused by their own defects. It is not effective until the buyer notifies the seller of it.

(3) A buyer who so revokes has the same rights and duties with regard to the goods involved as if he had rejected them. (5A Del. C. 1953, § 2-608; 55 Del. Laws, c. 349.)

RULE §2-608: Revocation of Acceptance:

(1) When Buyer May Revoke: The Buyer may revoke his acceptance if:
- **i) A non-conformity *substantially impairs* the value of the goods to the Buyer; and**
- **ii) Either:**
  - **(a) He has accepted the goods assuming that the Seller would cure the non-conformity, but the Seller neglected to do so *seasonably;* or**
  - **(b) He accepted the goods without knowing of the non-conformity either because:**
    - **1. It was difficult to discover the non-conformity before acceptance; or**
    - **2. The Seller's assurances induced him to accept**

(2) Time of Revocation:
- **a) Revocation of acceptance must occur within a reasonable time:**
  - **1. After the Buyer discovers *or should have discovered* the non-conformity; and**
  - **2. Before there is any *substantial change* in the condition of the goods (which is not caused by their own defects)**
- **b) Revocation is not effective until the Buyer notifies the Seller of it.**

(3) Effect of Revocation: A Buyer who properly revokes has the same rights and duties as if he had rejected them.

§ 2-609. Right to adequate assurance of performance.

(1) A contract for sale imposes an obligation on each party that the other's expectation of receiving due performance will not be impaired. When reasonable grounds for insecurity arise with respect to the performance of either party the other may in

writing demand adequate assurance of due performance and until he receives such assurance may if commercially reasonable suspend any performance for which he has not already received the agreed return.

(2) Between merchants the reasonableness of grounds for insecurity and the adequacy of any assurance offered shall be determined according to commercial standards.

(3) Acceptance of any improper delivery or payment does not prejudice the aggrieved party's right to demand adequate assurance of future performance.

(4) After receipt of a justified demand failure to provide within a reasonable time not exceeding thirty days such assurance of due performance as is adequate under the circumstances of the particular case is a repudiation of the contract. (5A Del. C. 1953, § 2-609; 55 Del. Laws, c. 349.)

RULE §2-609: Right to Adequate Assurance of Performance:

(1) Adequate Assurance:

- ***a) A contract for sale creates an obligation in each party to maintain the other party's expectations of due performance.***
- ***b) A party will be excused from performing any contractual obligation if:***
    - ***1) The party had reasonable grounds of insecurity as to whether the other party will perform according to the contract; and***
    - ***2) The party sends a written notice to the other party demanding adequate assurance of due performance; and***
    - ***3) The other party did not yet respond to the demand; and***
    - ***4) It is commercially reasonable to suspend such Performance; and***
    - ***5) The party did not receive payment (or other return) for the obligations it plans to suspend.***
- ***c) <u>Parties:</u>***
    - ***1) "Repudiating Party" - The party failing to give adequate assurance of performance***
    - ***2) 'Aggrieved Party" - The party demanding assurance***

of performance

(2) Standards: The following terms shall be construed according to commercial standards if the contract is between Merchants:
- ***a) "Reasonable Grounds for Insecurity"***
- ***b) "Adequacy of assurance"***

(3) Installments: A party is not precluded from demanding adequate assurance of future obligations even if he accepted an improper delivery or payment of earlier obligations.

(4) Repudiation: A party who fails to provide adequate assurance (under the circumstances of the case) to a justified demand within a reasonable amount of time (no more than 30 days) will have repudiated the contract.

§ 2-610. Anticipatory repudiation.

When either party repudiates the contract with respect to a performance not yet due the loss of which will substantially impair the value of the contract to the other, the aggrieved party may

(a) for a commercially reasonable time await performance by the repudiating party; or

(b) resort to any remedy for breach (Section 2-703 or Section 2-711), even though he has notified the repudiating party that he would await the latter's performance and has urged retraction; and

(c) in either case suspend his own performance or proceed in accordance with the provisions of this Article on the seller's right to identify goods to the contract notwithstanding breach or to salvage unfinished goods (Section 2-704). (5A Del. C. 1953, § 2-610; 55 Del. Laws, c. 349.)

RULE §2-610: Anticipatory Repudiation:

1. "Anticipatory Repudiation" - Anticipatory Repudiation occurs when:
   a. Either party repudiates the contract (see §2-609); and
   b. The repudiated portion of the contract is not yet due; and
   c. The loss of such performance will substantially impair the value of the contract

2. Rights of Aggrieved Party upon Anticipatory Repudiation: The aggrieved party may:
   (a) <u>Await Performance</u> - from the repudiating party, for a commercially reasonable time or
   (b) <u>Resort to Breach Remedies</u> (as per §2-703 (for Seller) or §2-711 (for Buyer)) - even if he told the repudiating party that he will wait for performance (subsection (a)); or
   (c) <u>Suspend Performance</u> - The aggrieved party may suspend his own performance.; or
   (d) <u>Identify and Salvage Goods</u> - The Seller may identify goods to a contract or salvage unfinished goods (as per §2-704).

§ 2-611. Retraction of anticipatory repudiation.

(1) Until the repudiating party's next performance is due he can retract his repudiation unless the aggrieved party has since the repudiation cancelled or materially changed his position or otherwise indicated that he considers the repudiation final.

(2) Retraction may be by any method which clearly indicates to the aggrieved party that the repudiating party intends to perform, but must include any assurance justifiably demanded under the provisions of this Article (Section 2-609).

(3) Retraction reinstates the repudiating party's rights under the contract with due excuse and allowance to the aggrieved party for any delay occasioned by the repudiation. (5A Del. C. § 2-611; 55 Del. Laws, c. 349.)

RULE §2-611: Retraction of Anticipatory Repudiation:

(1) Time for Retraction: The repudiating party may retract his repudiation if:
- ***a) His next performance is still not yet due; and***
- ***b) The aggrieved party has not:***
  - ***1. Canceled the contract; or***
  - ***2. Materially changed its position; or***
  - ***3. Otherwise indicated that it considers the repudiation final***

(2) Requirements for Retraction: A valid retraction of repudiation must:
- ***a) Clearly indicate to the aggrieved party that the repudiating party intends to perform; and***
- ***b) Include any adequate assurance justifiably demanded under §2-609***

(3) Effect of Retraction:
- ***a) The repudiating party's rights under the contract are reinstated; and***
- ***b) The aggrieved party is excused for any delay due to the repudiation.***

§ 2-612. "Installment contract"; breach.

(1) An "installment contract" is one which requires or authorizes the delivery of goods in separate lots to be separately accepted, even though the contract contains a clause "each delivery is a separate contract" or its equivalent.

(2) The buyer may reject any installment which is non-conforming if the non-conformity substantially impairs the value of that installment and cannot be cured or if the non-conformity is a defect in the required documents; but if the non-conformity does not fall within subsection (3) and the seller gives adequate assurance of its cure the buyer must accept that installment.

(3) Whenever non-conformity or default with respect to one or more installments substantially impairs the value of the whole contract there is a breach of the whole. But the aggrieved party reinstates the contract if he accepts a non-conforming installment

without seasonably notifying of cancellation or if he brings an action with respect only to past installments or demands performance as to future installments. (5A Del. C. 1953, § 2-612; 55 Del. Laws, c. 349.)

RULE §2-612: Installment Contract Breaches:

(1) "Installment Contract" – a contract which recognizes or authorizes the delivery of goods in Separate lots to be separately accepted (even if the contract says that each delivery is considered a separate contract).

(2) Rejecting Installments:
- ***a) The Buyer may reject any installment which is non-conforming if:***
  - ***1) The non-conformity substantially impairs the value of the installment; and***
  - ***2) Either:***
    - ***a. The defect cannot be cured; or***
    - ***b. The defect is in the documents and not the goods themselves***
- ***b) The buyer must accept the goods if the Seller gives adequate assurance that he will fix the defects***

(3) Substantial non-conformity:
- ***a) A substantial non-conformity of one or more installments is considered to be a breach of the entire contract.***
- ***b) The Buyer may reinstate an Installment Contract if he:***
  - ***1) Accepts a non-conforming installment without seasonably notifying the Seller of cancellation; or***
  - ***2) Brings an action only against past installments; or***
  - ***3) Demands performance as to future installments (not present, non-conforming installment)***

§ 2-613. Casualty to identified goods.

Where the contract requires for its performance goods identified when the contract is made, and the goods suffer casualty without fault of either party before the risk of loss passes to the buyer, or in a proper case under a "no arrival, no sale" term (Section 2-324) then

(a) if the loss is total the contract is avoided; and

(b) if the loss is partial or the goods have so deteriorated as no longer to conform to the contract the buyer may nevertheless demand inspection and at his option either treat the contract as avoided or accept the goods with due allowance from the contract price for the deterioration or the deficiency in quantity but without further right against the seller. (5A Del. C. 1953, § 2-613; 55 Del. Laws, c. 349.)

RULE §2-613: Casualty to Identified Goods:

(a) Total Loss: A contract may be avoided if:

- ***1) The contract requires that the goods be identified when the contract is made; and***
- ***2) All of the identified goods suffer from a casualty; and***
- ***3) The casualty is not the fault of either party; and***
- ***4) Either:***
  - ***a) The risk of loss did not yet pass to the Buyer; or***
  - ***b) The contract was a "No Arrival, No Sale" contract (as per §2-324 (in a proper case))***

(b) Partial Loss or Deteriorated Goods:

- ***1) The Buyer has the option of avoiding or accepting the contract if:***
  - ***a) The contract requires that the goods be identified when the contract is made; and***
  - ***b) Either:***
    - ***1. Some of the identified goods suffer from a casualty; or***
    - ***2. The goods have deteriorated so much that they do not conform to the contract***
  - ***and c) The casualty is not the fault of either party***
  - ***and d) Either:***
    - ***1. The risk of loss did not yet pass to the Buyer; or***
    - ***2. The contract was a "No Arrival, No Sale" contract (as per §2-324)***

2) <u>Accepting Goods at a Discount:</u>

a) The Buyer may accept the goods and receive a discount for the deterioration or deficiency in the goods.

b) If the Buyer receives such a discount he will not have any other rights against the Seller.

§ 2-614. Substituted performance.

(1) Where without fault of either party the agreed berthing, loading, or unloading facilities fail or an agreed type of carrier becomes unavailable or the agreed manner of delivery otherwise becomes commercially impracticable but a commercially reasonable substitute is available, such substitute performance must be tendered and accepted.

(2) If the agreed means or manner of payment fails because of domestic or foreign governmental regulation, the seller may withhold or stop delivery unless the buyer provides a means or manner of payment which is commercially a substantial equivalent. If delivery has already been taken, payment by the means or in the manner provided by the regulation discharges the buyer's obligation unless the regulation is discriminatory, oppressive or predatory. (5A Del. C. 1953, § 2-614; 55 Del. Laws, c. 349.)

RULE §2-614: Substituted Performance:

(1) Substitute Delivery: Substitute Performance must be <u>Tendered</u> and <u>Accepted</u> if:

a) <u>Either:</u>

1. The agreed berthing, loading or unloading facilities fail; or

2. An agreed type of Carrier becomes unavailable; or

3. The agreed upon manner of delivery otherwise becomes commercially impracticable

and b) A commercially reasonable substitute is available

and c) Neither party is at fault

(2) Substitute Payment:

a) <u>Before Delivery Begins:</u>

The Seller may <u>Withhold</u> or <u>Stop</u> <u>Delivery</u> if:

1) The Agreed upon means or manner of payment fails (due to foreign or domestic governmental regulations); and

2) The Buyer does not provide a commercially substantial equivalent manner of payment

b) <u>After Delivery Begins:</u> The Buyer's obligation to pay the Seller will be discharged if:

1) Payment is made in the manner provided for by the governmental regulations; and

2) Such regulations are not discriminatory, oppressive, or predatory.

§ 2-615. Excuse by failure of presupposed conditions.

Except so far as a seller may have assumed a greater obligation and subject to the preceding section on substituted performance:

(a) Delay in delivery or non-delivery in whole or in part by a seller who complies with paragraphs (b) and (c) is not a breach of his duty under a contract for sale if performance as agreed has been made impracticable by the occurrence of a contingency the non-occurrence of which was a basic assumption on which the contract was made or by compliance in good faith with any applicable foreign or domestic governmental regulation or order whether or not it later proves to be invalid.

(b) Where the causes mentioned in paragraph (a) affect only a part of the seller's capacity to perform, he must allocate production and deliveries among his customers but may at his option include regular customers not then under contract as well as his own requirements for further manufacture. He may so allocate in any manner which is fair and reasonable.

(c) The seller must notify the buyer seasonably that there will be delay or non-delivery and, when allocation is required under paragraph (b), of the estimated quota thus made available for the buyer. (5A Del. C. 1953, § 2-615; 55 Del. Laws, c. 349.)

RULE § 2-615: Excuse by Failure of Presupposed Conditions: ("Commercial Impracticability")

(a) Delay In Delivery/Non-Delivery:

The Seller is not considered to have breached its contract if he delays delivery or fails to deliver goods (in whole or in part) if:

1. The Seller had complied with (b) and (c) below; and
2. The agreed upon manner of performance has become impracticable, either by
   a. The occurrence a certain event, if the contract was made with the basic assumption that such an event would not occur; or
   b. Good Faith compliance with any foreign or domestic governmental regulation or order (whether or not it later proves to be invalid)

(b) Diminished Number of Goods:
1. <u>Allocation of Goods:</u> If the causes in (a) (above) affect only part of the Seller's capacity to perform (by reducing the amount of goods he has to ship) the Seller must allocate production and delivery of the goods among all of his customers.
2. <u>Guidelines for Allocation:</u> The Seller must allocate the goods according to these guidelines (in any manner which is fair and reasonable):
   a) The Seller does not have to allocate the goods only to customers with outstanding orders.
   b) The Seller may allocate goods to "regular customers," even though they do not have outstanding orders for goods.
   c) The Seller may allocate goods for his own requirements or for future manufacture.

(c) Notice to the Buyer:
1. The Seller must seasonably notify the Buyer of the delay or non-delivery.
2. If the Seller will be allocating goods (as per (b) above), he must seasonably notify the Buyer of the estimated quantity he will be shipping.

(d) This Section is subject to §2-614 and to any "greater" obligation which the Seller may assume.

§ 2-616. Procedure on notice claiming excuse.

(1) Where the buyer receives notification of a material or indefinite delay or an allocation justified under the preceding section he may by written notification to the seller as to any delivery concerned, and where the prospective deficiency substantially impairs the value of the whole contract under the provisions of this Article relating to breach of installment contracts (Section 2-612), then also as to the whole,

(a) terminate and thereby discharge any unexecuted portion of the contract; or

(b) modify the contract by agreeing to take his available quota in substitution.

(2) If after receipt of such notification from the seller the buyer fails so to modify the contract within a reasonable time not exceeding thirty days the contract lapses with respect to any deliveries affected.

(3) The provisions of this section may not be negated by agreement except in so far as the seller has assumed a greater obligation under the preceding section. (5A Del. C. 1953, § 2-616; 55 Del. Laws, c. 349.)

RULE §2-616: Procedure for Notice Claiming Excuse:

(1) Buyer's Rights Upon Seller's Excuse:

i) Applicability: This section shall only apply if:

a) The Buyer receives a notice that either

1. There will be a material or indefinite delay in delivery; or

2. The Seller will be allocating goods (as per §2-615(b)), and shipping the Buyer a smaller quantity than he originally ordered.

and b) The deficiency in the amount of goods substantially impairs the value of the whole contract (as per §2-612); and

c) The Buyer sends a written notice of its intentions

ii) Buyer's Rights: If the above conditions are fulfilled, the Buyer may choose to either:

(a) Terminate the Whole Contract - and discharge any unexecuted portion of the contract; or

(b) Modify the Contract - by agreeing to take the Seller's

available quantity of goods as substitution

(2) The contract will lapse (with respect to any deliveries affected) if:
- ***a) The Buyer receives such notice of delay or allocation; and***
- ***b) The Buyer fails to modify the contract within a reasonable time (no more than <u>30 Days)</u>***

(3) The provisions of this section may not be negated by agreement unless the Seller has assumed a greater obligation under §2-615.

UNIFORM COMMERCIAL CODE

ARTICLE 2 - SALES

PART 7

Remedies

§ 2-701. Remedies for breach of collateral contracts not impaired.

Remedies for breach of any obligation or promise collateral or ancillary to a contract for sale are not impaired by the provisions of this Article. (5A Del. C. 1953, § 2-701; 55 Del. Laws, c. 349.)

RULE §2-701: Remedies for Breach of Collateral Contracts Not Impaired:

Article 2 does not limit remedies for breach of any obligation or promise (collateral or ancillary) to a contract for sale.

§ 2-702. Seller's remedies on discovery of buyer's insolvency.

(1) Where the seller discovers the buyer to be insolvent he may refuse delivery except for cash including payment for all goods theretofore delivered under the contract, and stop delivery under this Article (Section 2-705).

(2) Where the seller discovers that the buyer has received goods on credit while insolvent he may reclaim the goods upon demand made within ten days after the receipt, but if misrepresentation of solvency has been made to the particular seller in writing within three months before delivery the ten day limitation does not apply. Except as provided in this subsection the seller may not base a right to reclaim goods on the buyer's fraudulent or innocent misrepresentation of solvency or of intent to pay.

(3) The seller's right to reclaim under subsection (2) is subject to the rights of a buyer in ordinary course or other good faith purchaser or lien creditor under this Article (Section 2-403). Successful reclamation of goods excludes all other remedies with respect to them. (5A Del. C. 1953, § 2-702; 55 Del. Laws, c. 349.)

RULE §2-702: Buyer's Insolvency; Reclamation Rights:

(1) Seller Discovers Buyer's Insolvency Before Delivery:
If the Seller discovers that the Buyer is insolvent, the Seller may:
a. Refuse to continue delivering unless Buyer promises to
1. Pay Cash on Delivery (C.O.D.); and
2. Pay for all shipments already delivered under the contract
and b. Stop delivery (as per §2-705)

(2) Buyer Receives Goods on Credit While Insolvent: If the Seller discovers that the Buyer has been receiving goods on credit while he was insolvent, the Seller may Reclaim the goods:
<u>Reclamation Requirements:</u>
1. 10 Day Time Limit - In order to reclaim the goods, the Seller must:
a) Demand payment or reclamation of the goods
b) Make the Demand within <u>10 Days</u> after the Buyer receives the goods
2. EXCEPTION - Written Misrepresentation of Solvency: 10 Day limit does not apply if the Buyer made a <u>Misrepresentation of Solvency:</u>
a) In Writing; and
b) Within <u>3 Months</u> before Delivery
3. The Seller may not base a right to reclaim the goods based on the Buyer's Fraudulent or Innocent misrepresentation of <u>Solvency</u> or <u>Intent to pay,</u> except as provided in this subsection (i.e. it must be in writing, within 3 Months before delivery).

(3) Limitations on the Seller's Rights to Reclaim:
a. The Seller's rights to reclaim are subject to the rights of:
1. A Buyer In the Ordinary Course (Bloc); and
2. Any other Good Faith Purchaser (under §2-403)
b. <u>Exclusion of Other Remedies:</u> Successful reclamation of goods excludes all other remedies (with respect to the reclaimed goods).

§ 2-703. Seller's remedies in general.

Where the buyer wrongfully rejects or revokes acceptance of goods or fails to make a payment due on or before delivery or repudiates with respect to a part or the whole, then with respect to any goods directly affected and, if the breach is of the whole contract (Section 2-612), then also with respect to the whole undelivered balance, the aggrieved seller may

(a) withhold delivery of such goods;

(b) stop delivery by any bailee as hereafter provided (Section 2-705);

(c) proceed under the next section respecting goods still unidentified to the contract;

(d) resell and recover damages as hereafter provided (Section 2-706);

(e) recover damages for non-acceptance (Section 2-708) or in a proper case the price (Section 2-709);

(f) cancel. (5A Del. C. 1953, § 2-703; 55 Del. Laws, c. 349.)

RULE §2-703: Seller's Remedies in General

1. <u>Seller is entitled to remedies when:</u>

- ***a. The Buyer wrongfully rejects goods; or***
- ***b. The Buyer wrongfully revokes acceptance of goods; or***
- ***c. The Buyer repudiates with respect to the whole or a part of the contract; or***
- ***d. The Buyer fails to make a payment due on or before delivery; Failure to make a payment includes (official comment 3):***
    - ***a. The dishonor of a check on due presentment***
    - ***b. The non-acceptance of a draft***
    - ***c. The failure to furnish an agreed letter of credit***

2. <u>The Seller's remedies apply with respect to:</u>

a. Any goods directly affected; and

b. If the breach is of the whole contract (§2-612), then also with respect to the whole undelivered balance

3. <u>Remedies Available - The Seller may:</u>

(a) Withhold delivery of the goods; or

(b) Stop delivery by any Bailee (as per §2-705); or

(c) Identify or salvage unfinished or unidentified goods (under §2-704); or (d) Resell and recover damages as provided in §2-706; or

(e) Recover damages for non-acceptance (§2-708) or in a proper case the price (§2-709); or

(f) Cancel the contract

§ 2-704. Seller's right to identify goods to the contract notwithstanding breach or to salvage unfinished goods.

(1) An aggrieved seller under the preceding section may

(a) identify to the contract conforming goods not already identified if at the time he learned of the breach they are in his possession or control;

(b) treat as the subject of resale goods which have demonstrably been intended for the particular contract even though those goods are unfinished.

(2) Where the goods are unfinished an aggrieved seller may in the exercise of reasonable commercial judgment for the purposes of avoiding loss and of effective realization either complete the manufacture and wholly identify the goods to the contract or cease manufacture and resale for scrap or salvage value or proceed in any other reasonable manner. (5A Del. C. 1953, § 2-704; 55 Del. Laws, c. 349.)

RULE §2-704: Seller's Right to Identify Goods to the Contract Notwithstanding Breach or to Salvage Unfinished Goods:

(1) <u>Rights of Aggrieved Seller under §2-703 may:</u>

(a) Conforming Finished Goods: Identify to the contract goods which have not yet been identified if:

1. The goods conform to the contract; and

2. At the time the Seller learned of the breach they are in the Seller's possession or control (the goods are then available for resale under §2-706 (official comment))

(b) Unfinished Goods: Resell goods which have clearly been intended for the particular contract (even though those goods are unfinished).

(2) <u>Seller's Remedies Where Goods are Unfinished:</u>

a. Where the goods are unfinished an aggrieved Seller may either:

1. Complete the manufacture and wholly identify the goods to the contract; or

2. Cease manufacture and resell them for scrap or salvage value; or

3. Proceed in any other reasonable manner

b. The Seller must exercise reasonable commercial judgment (the burden is on the Buyer to show otherwise) for the purposes of:

1. Avoiding loss; and

2. Effective realization

§ 2-705. Seller's stoppage of delivery in transit or otherwise.

(1) The seller may stop delivery of goods in the possession of a carrier or other bailee when he discovers the buyer to be insolvent (Section 2-702) and may stop delivery of carload, truckload, planeload or larger shipments of express or freight when the buyer repudiates or fails to make a payment due before delivery or if for any other reason the seller has a right to withhold or reclaim the goods.

(2) As against such buyer the seller may stop delivery until

(a) receipt of the goods by the buyer; or

(b) acknowledgment to the buyer by any bailee of the goods except a carrier that the bailee holds the goods for the buyer; or

(c) such acknowledgment to the buyer by a carrier by reshipment or as warehouseman; or

(d) negotiation to the buyer of any negotiable document of title covering the goods.

(3)(a) To stop delivery the seller must so notify as to enable the bailee by reasonable diligence to prevent delivery of the goods.

(b) After such notification the bailee must hold and deliver the goods according to the directions of the seller but the seller is liable to the bailee for any ensuing charges or damages.

(c) If a negotiable document of title has been issued for goods the bailee is not obliged to obey a notification to stop until surrender of the document.

(d) A carrier who has issued a non-negotiable bill of lading is not obliged to obey a notification to stop received from a person other than the consignor. (5A Del. C. 1953, § 2-705; 55 Del. Laws, c. 349.)

§2-705: Seller's Stoppage of Delivery in Transit or Otherwise:

(1) Seller's Right To Stop Delivery:

- ***a. Insolvency: The Seller may stop delivery of goods in the possession of a Carrier or other Bailee when he discovers the Buyer to be insolvent (§2-702).***
- ***b. Other Situations: The Seller may stop delivery of carload, truckload, planeload or larger shipments of express or freight when:***
    - ***1. The Buyer repudiates; or***
    - ***2. If for any other reason the Seller has a right to withhold or reclaim the goods; or***
    - ***3. The Buyer fails to make a payment due before delivery; Failure to make a payment includes (official comment 3):***

a. The dishonor of a check on due presentment
b. The non-acceptance of a draft
c. The failure to furnish an agreed letter of credit

(2) <u>Seller's Time Limit:</u> The Seller may stop delivery until:
(a) The Buyer receives the goods (this includes receipt by the Buyer's designated representative, the sub-purchaser, when shipment is made direct to him and the Buyer himself never receives the goods (official comment)); or
(b) A Bailee of the goods (except a Carrier) acknowledges to the Buyer that the goods are being held for the Buyer; or
(c) The Carrier acknowledges that the goods are being held for the Buyer, <u>either:</u>
1. By reshipment (this does not include diversion of a shipment when it is merely an incident to the original contract of transportation or does not change the destination (official comment)); or
2. As a Warehouseman (this requires a contract of a truly different character from the original shipment, a contract not in extension of transit but as a Warehouseman (official comment))
or (d) Negotiation to the Buyer of any negotiable document of title covering the goods.

(3) <u>Stopping Delivery:</u>
(a) Notice: To stop delivery the Seller must give the Bailee notice in order to enable him to prevent delivery by reasonable diligence.

(b) Seller's and Bailee's Responsibilities: After such notification:
1. The Bailee must hold and deliver the goods according to the directions of the Seller.
2. The Seller is liable to the Bailee for any ensuing charges or damages.

(c) Bailee to Stop Delivery: If a negotiable document of title

has been issued for goods the Bailee is not obliged to obey a notification to stop delivery until surrender of the document (a Bailee is under no duty to recognize the stop order of a stranger to the Carrier's contract (official comment)).

(d) Carrier to Stop Delivery: A Carrier who has issued a non-negotiable Bill of Lading is not obliged to obey a notification to stop delivery unless he is notified by the Consignor (a Bailee is under no duty to recognize the stop order of a stranger to the Carrier's contract (official comment)).

§ 2-706. Seller's resale including contract for resale.

(1) Under the conditions stated in Section 2-703 on seller's remedies, the seller may resell the goods concerned or the undelivered balance thereof. Where the resale is made in good faith and in a commercially reasonable manner the seller may recover the difference between the resale price and the contract price together with any incidental damages allowed under the provisions of this Article (Section 2-710), but less expenses saved in consequence of the buyer's breach.

(2) Except as otherwise provided in subsection (3) or unless otherwise agreed resale may be at public or private sale including sale by way of one or more contracts to sell or of identification to an existing contract of the seller. Sale may be as a unit or in parcels and at any time and place and on any terms but every aspect of the sale including the method, manner, time, place and terms must be commercially reasonable. The resale must be reasonably identified as referring to the broken contract, but it is not necessary that the goods be in existence or that any or all of them have been identified to the contract before the breach.

(3) Where the resale is at private sale the seller must give the buyer reasonable notification of his intention to resell.

(4) Where the resale is at public sale

(a) only identified goods can be sold except where there is a recognized market for a public sale of futures in goods of the kind; and

(b) it must be made at a usual place or market for public sale if one is reasonably available and except in the case of goods which are perishable or threaten to decline in value speedily the seller must give the buyer reasonable notice of the time and place of the resale; and

(c) if the goods are not to be within the view of those attending the sale the notification of sale must state the place where the goods are located and provide for their reasonable inspection by prospective bidders; and

(d) the seller may buy.

(5) A purchaser who buys in good faith at a resale takes the goods free of any rights of the original buyer even though the seller fails to comply with one or more of the requirements of this section.

(6) The seller is not accountable to the buyer for any profit made on any resale. A person in the position of a seller (Section 2-707) or a buyer who has rightfully rejected or justifiably revoked acceptance must account for any excess over the amount of his security interest, as hereinafter defined (subsection (3) of Section 2-711). (5A Del. C. 1953, § 2-706; 55 Del. Laws, c. 349.)

RULE §2-706: Seller's Resale Including Contract For Resale:

(1) <u>Resale By Seller for Buyer's Breach or Insolvency:</u>

a. Seller's Right: Under the conditions stated in §2-703 (breach or insolvency), the Seller may:

1. Resell the goods concerned; or

2. Resell the undelivered balance of the goods

b. <u>Seller Damages Recoverable:</u> The Seller may recover:

The resale price - The contract price + Any incidental damages (allowed under §2-710) - Expenses saved in consequence of the Buyer's breach

c. <u>Requirements:</u> to recover damages, Seller has to resell:

1. In good faith; and

2. In a commercially reasonable manner

(2) <u>Method of Resale:</u>

a. General Notes:

1. Every aspect of the sale including the <u>method, manner,</u> time, <u>place</u> and <u>terms</u> must be commercially reasonable.
2. The resale must be reasonably identified as referring to the broken contract, but it is not necessary for:
i. The goods to be in existence; or
ii. Any or all of the goods to have been identified to the contract before the breach. 3. Terms of resale are subject to:
(i) §2-706(3); and
(ii) Agreement otherwise by parties.

b. Type of Sale - Depending on commercial reasonableness, resale may be at:
1. Public sale (auction); or
2. Private sale (ex: solicitation and negotiation conducted either directly or through a broker)

c. This section includes sale by way of:
1. One or more contracts to sell; or
2. Identification to an existing contract of the Seller d. Units of Sale - Sale may be:
1. As a unit; or
2. In parcels

e. Time and Place - Sale may be at any time and place and on any terms.

(3) <u>Private Resale</u> - Where the resale is at private sale the Seller must give the Buyer reasonable notification of his intention to resell (notification of the time and place of this type of sale is not required).

(4) <u>Public Resale</u> - Where the resale is at public sale:
(a) <u>Type of Goods That Can Be Sold:</u>
1. Only identified goods can be sold.
2. Futures Market Exception: Where there is a recognized market for a public sale of futures in goods of the kind.
(b) <u>Seller's Requirements:</u>
1. Place: The auction must be made at a usual

place or market for public sale (which prospective bidders may reasonably be expected to attend).

2. Notice:

a. The Seller must give the Buyer reasonable notice of the time and place so that he may:

i. Bid; or

ii. Secure the attendance of other bidders

b. Perishable Goods Exception: In the case of goods "which are perishable or threaten to decline speedily in value, " notice is not required.

(c) <u>Goods Not Present at Sale</u> - If the goods are not to be within the view of those attending the sale:

1. The notification of sale must <u>state the place</u> where the goods are located; and

2. The notification must provide for <u>reasonable inspection</u> of the goods by prospective bidders

(d) The Seller may buy (his own goods) at the sale.

(5) <u>Purchaser's Rights:</u> A purchaser who buys in good faith at a resale takes the goods <u>free of any rights of the original Buyer</u> (even though the Seller fails to comply with one or more of the requirements of this section).

(6) <u>Profits:</u>

a. The Seller retains profit, if any, made on any resale.

b. A person in the position of a Seller (as per §2-707) must give any excess (above his "security interest" as defined in §2-711(3)) to the Seller.

c. A Buyer who has rightfully rejected or justifiably revoked acceptance must also give any "profits" to the Seller (i.e. the difference between the sale price and the Seller's "security interest" in the goods (as defined in §2-711(3)).

§ 2-707. "Person in the position of a seller."

(1) A "person in the position of a seller" includes as against a principal an agent who has paid or become responsible for the price of goods on behalf of his principal or anyone who otherwise holds a security interest or other right in goods similar to that of a seller.

(2) A person in the position of a seller may as provided in this Article withhold or stop delivery (Section 2-705) and resell (Section 2-706) and recover incidental damages (Section 2-710). (5A Del. C. 1953, § 2-707; 55 Del. Laws, c. 349.)

RULE §2-707: "Person in the Position of a Seller"

(1) A "Person In The Position of a Seller" includes:

- ***a. An agent who has paid or become responsible for the price of goods on behalf of his principal; or***
- ***b. Anyone who otherwise holds a security interest or other right in goods similar to that of a Seller***

(2) A person in the position of a Seller may:

- ***a. Withhold or stop delivery (§2-705); and***
- ***b. Resell (§2-706); and***
- ***c. Recover incidental damages (§2-710)***

§ 2-708. Seller's damages for non-acceptance or repudiation.

(1) Subject to subsection (2) and to the provisions of this Article with respect to proof of market price (Section 2-723), the measure of damages for non-acceptance or repudiation by the buyer is the difference between the market price at the time and place for tender and the unpaid contract price together with any incidental damages provided in this Article (Section 2-710), but less expenses saved in consequence of the buyer's breach.

(2) If the measure of damages provided in subsection (1) is inadequate to put the seller in as good a position as performance would have done then the measure of

damages is the profit (including reasonable overhead) which the seller would have made from full performance by the buyer, together with any incidental damages provided in this Article (Section 2-710), due allowance for costs reasonably incurred and due credit for payments or proceeds of resale. (5A Del. C. 1953, § 2-708; 55 Del. Laws, c. 349.)

RULE §2-708: Seller's Damages for Non-acceptance or Repudiation:

(1) <u>Expectation Damages:</u> If the Buyer does not accept or repudiates, the Seller's damages are (subject to 2-708(2) and to §2-723 (proof of market price)):

The market price at the time and place for tender - The unpaid contract price + Any incidental damages provided in this Article (§2-710)- Expenses saved in consequence of the Buyer's breach

(2) <u>Lost Profit:</u> If the measure of damages in subsection (1) is not enough to put the Seller in as good a position as he would have been had the Buyer performed (i.e. the Seller is a "lost volume seller"), then the measure of damages is:

The profit ((including reasonable overhead) which the Seller would have made from full performance by the Buyer) + Any incidental damages provided in this Article (§2-710) + Due allowance for costs reasonably incurred + Due credit for payments or proceeds of resale

§ 2-709. Action for the price.

(1) When the buyer fails to pay the price as it becomes due the seller may recover, together with any incidental damages under the next section, the price

(a) of goods accepted or of conforming goods lost or damaged within a commercially reasonable time after risk of their loss has passed to the buyer; and

(b) of goods identified to the contract if the seller is unable after reasonable effort to resell them at a reasonable price or the circumstances reasonably indicate that such effort will be unavailing.

(2) Where the seller sues for the price he must hold for the buyer any goods which have been identified to the contract and are still in his control except that if resale becomes possible he may resell them at any time prior to the collection of the judgment. The net proceeds of any such resale must be credited to the buyer and payment of the judgment entitles him to any goods not resold.

(3) After the buyer has wrongfully rejected or revoked acceptance of the goods or has failed to make a payment due or has repudiated (Section 2-610), a seller who is held not entitled to the price under this section shall nevertheless be awarded damages for non-acceptance under the preceding section. (5A Del. C. 1953, § 2-709; 55 Del. Laws, c. 349.)

RULE §2-709: Action for the Price:

(1) Buyer Fails to Pay: When the Buyer fails to pay the price as it becomes due, the Seller may recover the following (+ any incidental damages under §2-710):

(a) Accepted/Destroyed Goods:

1. Accepted Goods - The price of the goods

2. Destroyed Goods - The price of the goods, if:

a. The goods were conforming goods; and

b. The goods were destroyed within a commercially reasonable time after risk of loss has passed to the Buyer

and (b) Identified Goods: The price of goods identified to the contract if:

1. The Seller is unable after reasonable effort to resell the goods at a reasonable price; or

2. The circumstances reasonably indicate that such effort will be unavailing

(2) Seller's Requirements With Respect to Identified Goods:

a. Seller must hold goods which have been identified to the contract for the Buyer if:

1. The Seller is suing the Buyer for their price; and

2. The goods are still in the Seller's control

b. Resale: If resale becomes possible, the Seller may resell the goods at any time before the judgment (price) is collected.

c. Buyer's Rights:

1. The net proceeds of any such resale must be credited to the Buyer.

2. Payment of the judgment entitles the Buyer to any goods not resold.

(3) Even if a Seller is not entitled to the price (under §2-709) he may be awarded damages for non-acceptance (under §2-708) if the Buyer:

a. Wrongfully rejected the goods; or

b. Wrongfully revoked acceptance of the goods; or

c. Has failed to make a payment due or d. Has repudiated (§2-610)

§ 2-710. Seller's incidental damages.

Incidental damages to an aggrieved seller include any commercially reasonable charges, expenses or commissions incurred in stopping delivery, in the transportation, care and custody of goods after the buyer's breach, in connection with return or resale of the goods or otherwise resulting from the breach. (5A Del. C. 1953, § 2-710; 55 Del. Laws, c. 349.)

RULE §2-710: Seller's Incidental Damages:

Incidental damages to an aggrieved Seller include any commercially reasonable charges, expenses or commissions:

1. Incurred in stopping delivery; or

2. Incurred in the transportation, care and custody of goods after the Buyer's breach; or

3. Incurred in connection with return or resale of the goods; or

4. Otherwise resulting from the breach

§ 2-711. Buyer's remedies in general; buyer's security interest in rejected goods.

(1) Where the seller fails to make delivery or repudiates or the buyer rightfully rejects or justifiably revokes acceptance then with respect to any goods involved, and with respect to the whole if the breach goes to the whole contract (Section 2-612), the buyer may cancel and whether or not he has done so may in addition to recovering so much of the price as has been paid

(a) "cover" and have damages under the next section as to all the goods, affected whether or not they have been identified to the contract; or

(b) recover damages for non-delivery as provided in this Article (Section 2-713).

(2) Where the seller fails to deliver or repudiates the buyer may also

(a) if the goods have been identified recover them as provided in this Article (Section 2-502); or

(b) in a proper case obtain specific performance or replevy the goods as provided in this Article (Section 2-716).

(3) On rightful rejection or justifiable revocation of acceptance a buyer has a security interest in goods in his possession or control for any payments made on their price and any expenses reasonably incurred in their inspection, receipt, transportation, care and custody and may hold such goods and resell them in like manner as an aggrieved seller (Section 2-706). (5A Del. C. 1953, § 2-711; 55 Del. Laws, c. 349.)

RULE § 2-711: Buyer's Remedies in General; Buyer's Security Interest in Rejected Goods:

Even though the Seller breached, the Buyer may be barred from using these remedies if.

a. The Seller properly tendered goods (as per §2-508); and
b. No delay was involved

(1) <u>Buyer's Remedies Permitting the Recovery of Money Damages:</u>

a. The Buyer is entitled to §2-711 remedies when:
1. The Seller fails to make delivery; or

2. The Seller repudiates; or
3. The Buyer rightfully rejects; or
4. The Buyer justifiably revokes acceptance

b. See §2-714 for remedies available to a Buyer if the goods were finally accepted.

c. The §2-711 remedies apply with respect to:
1. Any goods involved; and
2. The whole contract (if the breach goes to the whole contract (see 2-612))

d. Buyer's Remedies - The Buyer may:
1. Cancel the contract; and
2. Recover as much of the price as he has paid (whether or not he has canceled the contract)
and 3. Either:
(a) "Cover" and recover damages under §2-712 as to all the goods affected (whether or not they have been identified to the contract); or
(b) Recover damages for non-delivery under §2-713.

(2) <u>Additional Remedies Which Permit Reaching the Goods Themselves:</u>
a. Remedies - The Buyer may:
(a) Recover the goods under §2-502 if the goods have been identified; or
(b) In a proper case obtain <u>specific performance</u> or <u>replevy</u> the goods as per §2-716

b. These additional remedies apply when:
1. The Seller fails to deliver; or
2. The Seller repudiates

(3) <u>The Buyer's Security Interest In The Goods:</u>
a. The Buyer has a Security Interest in goods which are in his possession or control in the amount of:
1. That part of the price already paid by the Buyer; or
2. Any expenses reasonably incurred in inspection, receipt, transportation, care and custody of the

goods

b. The Buyer may hold and resell (§2-706) such goods. c. This subsection applies if:

1. The Buyer rightfully rejected the goods; or

2. The Buyer justifiably revoked acceptance of the goods

§ 2-712. "Cover"; buyer's procurement of substitute goods.

(1) After a breach within the preceding section the buyer may "cover" by making in good faith and without unreasonable delay any reasonable purchase of or contract to purchase goods in substitution for those due from the seller.

(2) The buyer may recover from the seller as damages the difference between the cost of cover and the contract price together with any incidental or consequential damages as hereinafter defined (Section 2-715), but less expenses saved in consequence of the seller's breach.

(3) Failure of the buyer to effect cover within this section does not bar him from any other remedy. (5A Del. C. 1953, § 2-712; 55 Del. Laws, c. 349.)

RULE §2-712: "Cover"; Buyer's Procurement of Substitute Goods:

(1) "Covering":

a. After a breach (within §2-711) the Buyer may "cover" by:

1. Making any reasonable purchase of goods to substitute those due from the Seller; or

2. Contracting to purchase such goods

b. Requirements - "Covering" must be done:

1. In good faith; and

2. Without unreasonable delay

c. Note: It is immaterial that hindsight may later prove that the method of cover used was not the cheapest or most effective.

(2) The Buyer may recover from the Seller the following as damages:

The cost of cover - The contract price + Any incidental or consequential damages (as defined in §2-715) - Expenses saved in consequence of the Seller's breach

(3) Failure of the Buyer to cover within §2-712 does not bar the Buyer from any other remedy. (Note: Cover is not a mandatory remedy for the Buyer. The Buyer is always free to choose between cover and damages for non-delivery under §2-713.)

Note: This subsection must be read in conjunction with §2-715. Moreover, the operation of §2-716 must be considered in this connection for availability of the goods to the particular Buyer for his particular needs is the test for that remedy and inability to cover is made an express condition to the right of the Buyer to replevy the goods.)

§ 2-713. Buyer's damages for non-delivery or repudiation.

(1) Subject to the provisions of this Article with respect to proof of market price (Section 2-723), the measure of damages for non-delivery or repudiation by the seller is the difference between the market price at the time when the buyer learned of the breach and the contract price together with any incidental and consequential damages provided in this Article (Section 2-715), but less expenses saved in consequence of the seller's breach.

(2) Market price is to be determined as of the place for tender or, in cases of rejection after arrival or revocation of acceptance, as of the place of arrival. (5A Del. C. 1953, § 2-713; 55 Del. Laws, c. 349.)

RULE §2-713: Buyer's Damages for Non-Delivery or Repudiation:

This section applies only when and to the extent that the Buyer has not covered.

(1) <u>Calculation of Damages</u> (Subject to §2-723) - The measure of damages for non-delivery or repudiation by the Seller is:

The market price (using the market in which the Buyer would have obtained cover and the price for goods of the same kind and in the same branch of trade) at the time when the Buyer learned of the breach - The contract price + Any incidental or consequential damages (as defined in §2-715) - Any expenses saved in consequence of the Seller's breach

(2) <u>"Market Price"</u> - The place where market price is to be determined is:

a. The place for tender (if the goods never reached their destination)
b. The place of arrival (if the goods are rejected or their acceptance is revoked after reaching their destination)

§ 2-714. Buyer's damages for breach in regard to accepted goods.

(1) Where the buyer has accepted goods and given notification (subsection (3) of Section 2-607) he may recover as damages for any non-conformity of tender the loss resulting in the ordinary course of events from the seller's breach as determined in any manner which is reasonable.

(2) The measure of damages for breach of warranty is the difference at the time and place of acceptance between the value of the goods accepted and the value they would have had if they had been as warranted, unless special circumstances show proximate damages of a different amount.

(3) In a proper case any incidental and consequential damages under the next section may also be recovered. (5A Del. C. 1953, § 2-714; 55 Del. Laws, c. 349.)

RULE §2-714: Buyer's Damages for Breach in Regard to Accented Goods:

(1) Remedy: The Buyer is permitted to recover his loss in any reasonable manner if:

- ***a. There is any non-conformity of tender (not only breaches of warranties but also any failure of the Seller to perform according to his obligations under the contract); and***
- ***b. The loss resulted from the ordinary course of events from the Seller's breach; and***
- ***c. The goods have been accepted; and***
- ***d. The time for revocation of acceptance has gone by; and***
- ***e. The Buyer gave notification (as per §2-607(3))***

(2) Damages for Breach of Warranty:

a. <u>Measure:</u> Damages for breach of Warranty equal:

The value of the goods accepted at the time and place of acceptance - The value they would have had if they had been as warranted

b. <u>Exception:</u> When special circumstances show proximate damages of a different amount.

(3) Incidental and Consequential Damages: In a proper case any incidental and consequential damages under §2-715 may also be recovered.

§ 2-715. Buyer's incidental and consequential damages.

(1) Incidental damages resulting from the seller's breach include expenses reasonably incurred in inspection, receipt, transportation and care and custody of goods rightfully rejected, any commercially reasonable charges, expenses or commissions in connection with effecting cover and any other reasonable expense incident to the delay or other breach.

(2) Consequential damages resulting from the seller's breach include

(a) any loss resulting from general or particular requirements and needs of which the seller at the time of contracting had reason to know and which could not reasonably be prevented by cover or otherwise; and

(b) injury to person or property proximately resulting from any breach of warranty. (5A Del. C. 1953, § 2-715; 55 Del. Laws, c. 349.)

RULE §2-715: Buyer's Incidental and Consequential Damages:

(1) Incidental Damages: Reimbursement for the Buyer's incidental damages resulting from the Seller's breach include:

- ***a. <u>Expenses for Rejected Goods:</u> Expenses reasonably incurred in inspection, receipt, transportation, care and custody of goods rightfully rejected; and***
- ***b. <u>Expenses for Covering:</u> Any commercially reasonable charges, expenses or commissions in connection with covering; and***
- ***c. <u>Expenses for Delay or Breach:</u> Any other reasonable expense incident to the delay or other breach***

(2) Consequential Damages: Consequential damages resulting from the Seller's breach include:

- ***(a) Loss: Any loss resulting from "general" or "particular" requirements:***
  - ***1. Conditions:***
    - ***a. The Seller had reason to know of the need for the requirement at the time of contracting; and***
    - ***b. The Buyer could not reasonably have prevented such losses by covering or otherwise***
  - ***2. Note:***
    - ***a. "Particular" needs of the Buyer must generally be made known to the Seller.***
    - ***b. "General" needs must rarely be made known to charge the Seller with knowledge.***

and (b) <u>Injury:</u> Injury to person or property proximately resulting from any breach of warranty

§ 2-716. Buyer's right to specific performance or replevin.

(1) Specific performance may be decreed where the goods are unique or in other proper circumstances.

(2) The decree for specific performance may include such terms and conditions as to payment of the price, damages, or other relief as the court may deem just.

(3) The buyer has a right of replevin for goods identified to the contract if after reasonable effort he is unable to effect cover for such goods or the circumstances reasonably indicate that such effort will be unavailing or if the goods have been shipped under reservation and satisfaction of the security interest in them has been made or tendered. In the case of goods bought for personal, family, or household purposes, the buyer's right of replevin vests upon acquisition of a special property, even if the seller had not then repudiated or failed to deliver. (5A Del. C. 1953, § 2-716; 55 Del. Laws, c. 349; 72 Del. Laws, c. 401, § 10.)

RULE §2-716: Buyer's Right to Specific Performance or Replevin:

(1) <u>Availability:</u> Specific performance may be decreed where:

- ***a. The goods are unique (The test is made in terms of the total situation which characterizes the contract, e.g., output and requirement contracts involving a particular or peculiarly available source or market); or***
- ***b. In other proper circumstances (Note: Inability to cover is evidence of "other proper circumstances")***

(2) <u>Terms of Specific Performance:</u> The decree for specific performance may specify terms and conditions relating to:

- ***a. Payment of the price; or***
- ***b. Payment of damages; or***
- ***c. Other relief as the court may deem just***

(3) <u>Replevin:</u> The Buyer has a right of replevin in cases in which:

a. Goods have been identified to the contract; and

b. <u>Either:</u>

1. Cover is not reasonably available; or

2. The circumstances reasonably indicate that an effort to cover will be unavailing; or

3. The goods have been shipped under reservation (i.e. the Seller shipped the goods while retaining a Security interest in them (as per §2-505)) and the Security Interest in the goods has been satisfied or tendered.

§ 2-717. Deduction of damages from the price.

The buyer on notifying the seller of his intention to do so may deduct all or any part of the damages resulting from any breach of the contract from any part of the price still due under the same contract. (5A Del. C. 1953, § 2-717; 55 Del. Laws, c. 349.)

RULE §2-717: Deduction of Damages from the Price:

a. The Buyer is permitted to deduct all or any part of the resulting damages from any part of the contract price still due if:

1. The Seller breaches; and

2. The Buyer gives notice of his intention to deduct all or part of the price

b. There is no formality of notice, and any language which reasonably indicates the Buyer's reason for holding up his payment is enough.

§ 2-718. Liquidation or limitation of damages; deposits.

(1) Damages for breach by either party may be liquidated in the agreement but only at an amount which is reasonable in the light of the anticipated or actual harm caused by the

breach, the difficulties of proof of loss, and the inconvenience or nonfeasibility of otherwise obtaining an adequate remedy. A term fixing unreasonably large liquidated damages is void as a penalty.

(2) Where the seller justifiably withholds delivery of goods because of the buyer's breach, the buyer is entitled to restitution of any amount by which the sum of his payments exceeds

(a) the amount to which the seller is entitled by virtue of terms liquidating the seller's damages in accordance with subsection (1), or

(b) in the absence of such terms, twenty per cent of the value of the total performance for which the buyer is obligated under the contract or $500, whichever is smaller.

(3) The buyer's right to restitution under subsection (2) is subject to offset to the extent that the seller establishes

(a) a right to recover damages under the provisions of this Article other than subsection (1), and

(b) the amount or value of any benefits received by the buyer directly or indirectly by reason of the contract.

(4) Where a seller has received payment in goods their reasonable value or the proceeds of their resale shall be treated as payments for the purposes of subsection (2); but if the seller has notice of the buyer's breach before reselling goods received in part performance, his resale is subject to the conditions laid down in this Article on resale by an aggrieved seller (Section 2-706). (5A Del. C. 1953, § 2-718; 55 Del. Laws, c. 349.)

RULE §2-718: Liquidation or Limitation of Damages; Restitution:

(1) Liquidated Damages Clauses:

- ***a. In an agreement, liquidated damage clauses for breach by either party are allowed.***
- ***b. <u>Requirement</u> - The amount involved has to be reasonable in the light of:***
  - ***1. The anticipated or actual harm caused by the breach; and***
  - ***2. The difficulties of proof of loss; and***

3. The inconvenience or non-feasibility of adequate compensation with another remedy

c. A term fixing unreasonably large liquidated damages is considered a "penalty" and is void.

(2) Restitution of Buyer's Payments: Where the Seller justifiably withholds delivery of goods because of the Buyer's breach, the Buyer may recover restitution in an amount equal to:

(a) <u>Liquidated Damages:</u>

Buyer's Payments - What the Seller is entitled to (in accordance with subsection (1))

or (b) If there are no liquidated damages clauses in the agreement for the Seller's damages, <u>the lower of:</u>

1. $500; or

2. Buyer's Payments - 20% of the value of the total performance (for which the Buyer is obligated under the contract)

(3) Reduction of Buyer's Restitution: The Buyer's right to recover under subsection (2) may be reduced by the amount the Seller establishes:

(a) A right to recover damages under Article 2 other than §2-718(1); or

(b) The amount or value of any benefits the Buyer received by reason of the contract (directly or indirectly)

(4) "Buyer's Payments": For purposes of subsection (2), the "Buyer's payments" includes:

a. The reasonable value of goods received by the Seller as payment (in part performance); or

b. 'The proceeds of their resale (provided the Seller does not have notice of the Buyer's breach before reselling the goods; if so, his resale is subject to the conditions in §2-706)

§ 2-719. Contractual modification or limitation of remedy.

(1) Subject to the provisions of subsections (2) and (3) of this section and of the preceding section on liquidation and limitation of damages,

(a) the agreement may provide for remedies in addition to or in substitution for those provided in this Article and may limit or alter the measure of damages recoverable under this Article, as by limiting the buyer's remedies to return of the goods and repayment of the price or to repair and replacement of non-conforming goods or parts; and

(b) resort to a remedy as provided is optional unless the remedy is expressly agreed to be exclusive, in which case it is the sole remedy.

(2) Where circumstances cause an exclusive or limited remedy to fail of its essential purpose, remedy may be had as provided in this title.

(3) Consequential damages may be limited or excluded unless the limitation or exclusion is unconscionable. Limitation of consequential damages for injury to the person in the case of consumer goods is prima facie unconscionable but limitation of damages where the loss is commercial is not. (5A Del. C. 1953, § 2-719; 55 Del. Laws, c. 349.)

RULE §2-719: Contractual Modification or Limitation of Remedy:

(1) Contractual Remedy Clauses: Subject to §2-719(2),(3) and §2-718, the contract may include other remedies:

(a) <u>These remedies include:</u>

1. Remedies in addition to Article 2 remedies; or

2. Remedies in substitution for Article 2 remedies; or

3. Changes/limitations on the measure of damages recoverable under Article 2, such as limiting the Buyer's remedies to:

a. Return of the goods and repayment of the price

b. Repair and replacement of non-conforming goods or parts

(b) <u>Effect on Other Remedies:</u>

1. These types of remedy clauses are optional rather than exclusive.

2. If the parties intend a clause to be the sole contract remedy, this must be clearly Expressed.

(2) Failure of §2-719 Remedies - The general Article 2 remedies will apply where an exclusive or limited remedy clause either:

a. Fails in its essential purpose because of the circumstances; or

b. Operates to deprive either party of the substantial value of the bargain (see official comment)

(3) Limitation of Consequential Damages:

a. Consequential damages may be limited or excluded unless the limitation or exclusion is unconscionable.

b. Consumer Damages: Limitation of consequential damages for injury to the person in the case of consumer goods is considered prima facie unconscionable.

c. Commercial Damages: Limitation of damages where the loss is commercial is not considered prima facie unconscionable.

§ 2-720. Effect of "cancellation" or "rescission" on claims for antecedent breach.

Unless the contrary intention clearly appears, expressions of "cancellation" or "rescission" of the contract or the like shall not be construed as a renunciation or discharge of any claim in damages for an antecedent breach. (5A Del. C. 1953, § 2-720; 55 Del. Laws, c. 349.)

RULE §2-720: Effect of "Cancellation" or "Rescission" on Claims for A Prior Breach:

"Cancellation" or "Rescission" of the contract (or similar

expressions) shall not be considered a renunciation or discharge of any claim in damages for a prior breach, unless the cancellation of the contract expressly declares that it discharges any rights.

§ 2-721. Remedies for fraud.

Remedies for material misrepresentation or fraud include all remedies available under this Article for non-fraudulent breach. Neither rescission or a claim for rescission of the contract for sale nor rejection or return of the goods shall bar or be deemed inconsistent with a claim for damages or other remedy. (5A Del. C. 1953, § 2-721; 55 Del. Laws, c. 349.)

RULE §2-721: Remedies for Fraud:

- ***a. Remedies for Material Misrepresentation or Fraud include all Article 2 remedies available for non-fraudulent breach.***
- ***b. The following do not bar other remedies or damages unless the circumstances of the case make the remedies incompatible:***
    - ***1. Rescission (or a claim for rescission) of the contract for fraud***
    - ***2. Rejection (or return) of the goods***

§ 2-722. Who can sue third parties for injury to goods.

Where a third party so deals with goods which have been identified to a contract for sale as to cause actionable injury to a party to that contract

(a) a right of action against the third party is in either party to the contract for sale who has title to or a security interest or a special property or an insurable interest in the goods; and if the goods have been destroyed or converted a right of action is also in the party who either bore the risk of loss under the contract for sale or has since the injury assumed that risk as against the other;

(b) if at the time of the injury the party plaintiff did not bear the risk of loss as against the other party to the contract for sale and there is no arrangement between them for disposition of the recovery, his suit or settlement is subject to his own interest, as a fiduciary for the other party to the contract;

(c) either party may with the consent of the other sue for the benefit of whom it may concern. (5A Del. C. 1953, § 2-722; 55 Del. Laws, c. 349.)

RULE §2-722: Who Can Sue Third Parties for Injury to Goods:

A third party can be sued if.

1. ***The third party causes injury to a party to a contract for sale; and***
2. ***The third party was dealing with goods which have been identified to the contract***

(a) Right to Sue Third Party: Either party to the contract for sale has a right to sue a third party if it:

1. ***Has title to the goods; or***
2. ***Has a security interest in the goods; or***
3. ***Has a special property interest; or***
4. ***Has an insurable interest in the goods; or***
5. ***If the goods have been destroyed or converted, and the party Either:***
    a. ***Bore the risk of loss under the contract for sale; or***
    b. ***Has assumed the other party's risk since the injury***

(b) The party plaintiff acts as a fiduciary for the other party of the contract in his suit or settlement (subject to his own interest), if:

1. ***The party plaintiff did not bear the other party's risk at the time of the injury; and***
2. ***There is no arrangement between them as to dividing the recovery***

(c) Either party may sue for any other concerned party's benefit if he receives consent to do so.

§ 2-723. Proof of market price; time and place.

(1) If an action based on anticipatory repudiation comes to trial before the time for performance with respect to some or all of the goods, any damages based on market price (Section 2-708 or Section 2-713) shall be determined according to the price of such goods prevailing at the time when the aggrieved party learned of the repudiation.

(2) If evidence of a price prevailing at the times or places described in this Article is not readily available the price prevailing within any reasonable time before or after the time described or at any other place which in commercial judgment or under usage of trade would serve as a reasonable substitute for the one described may be used, making any proper allowance for the cost of transporting the goods to or from such other place.

(3) Evidence of a relevant price prevailing at a time or place other than the one described in this Article offered by one party is not admissible unless and until he has given the other party such notice as the court finds sufficient to prevent unfair surprise. (5A Del. C. 1953, § 2-723; 55 Del. Laws, c. 349.)

RULE §2-723: Proof of Market Price: Time and Place:

(1) Trial Before Performance Time: If an Anticipatory Repudiation case comes to trial before the time for performance (with respect to some or all of the goods), the market price used for those goods (for purposes of §2-708 or §2-713 damages) is the price of those goods <u>at the time the aggrieved party learned of the repudiation.</u>

(2) Market Price Not Readily Available: When a market price is not readily available, the court may receive evidence of prices current in other comparable markets or at other times comparable to the one in question:

a. <u>Substitute for price prevailing at a particular time</u> - The price prevailing within any reasonable time before or after the time described.

b. ***Substitute for price prevailing at a particular place - The price prevailing at any other place which in commercial judgment or under usage of trade would as a reasonable substitute, accounting for the cost of transporting the goods to or from that place.***

(3) Evidence of Price:

a. A party may offer evidence as to a relevant price prevailing at a time or place other than the one described in this Article only if he has given the other party notice (to prevent unfair surprise).

b. The court uses its discretion to determine whether such evidence is admissible.

§ 2-724. Admissibility of market quotations.

Whenever the prevailing price or value of any goods regularly bought and sold in any established commodity market is in issue, reports in official publications or trade journals or in newspapers or periodicals of general circulation published as the reports of such market shall be admissible in evidence. The circumstances of the preparation of such a report may be shown to affect its weight but not its admissibility. (5A Del. C. 1953, § 2-724; 55 Del. Laws, c. 349.)

RULE §2-724: Admissibility of Market Quotations:

1. Admissibility: Market quotations are admissible when the price or value of goods regularly traded in any established market is in issue.

2. Sources of Quotations - These market quotes may be obtained from:

a. Reports in official publications or trade journals; or

b. Reports in newspapers or periodicals of general circulation published as market reports

3. Challenges Against the Quotations: The circumstances of the preparation of the reports may be shown in order to affect their weight as evidence, but not their admissibility.

§ 2-725. Statute of limitations in contracts for sale.

(1) An action for breach of any contract for sale must be commenced within 4 years after the cause of action has accrued. By the original agreement the parties may reduce the period of limitations to not less than one year but may not extend it.

(2) A cause of action accrues when the breach occurs, regardless of the aggrieved party's lack of knowledge of the breach. A breach of warranty occurs when tender of delivery is made, except that where a warranty explicitly extends to future performance of the goods and discovery of the breach must await the time of such performance the cause of action accrues when the breach is or should have been discovered.

(3) Where an action commenced within the time limited by subsection (1) is so terminated as to leave available a remedy by another action for the same breach such other action may be commenced after the expiration of the time limited and within 6 months after the termination of the first action unless the termination resulted from voluntary discontinuance or from dismissal for failure or neglect to prosecute.

(4) This section does not alter the law on tolling of the statute of limitations nor does it apply to causes of action which have accrued before this subtitle becomes effective. (5A Del. C. 1953, § 2-725; 55 Del. Laws, c. 349.)

RULE §2-725: Statute of Limitations in Contracts for Sale:

(1) Uniform Statute of Limitations in Contracts for Sale:

- ***a. Actions must be commenced within 4 years after the cause of action has accrued.***
- ***b. The parties may change the period of limitation in their original contract:***
    - ***1. The parties may reduce the period to a minimum of 1 year.***
    - ***2. The parties may not, however, extend the 4 year period.***

(2) Time of Accrual of Cause of Action:

- ***a. A cause of action is considered to have accrued when the breach Occurs (regardless of whether or not the aggrieved party knew of the breach).***
- ***b. A breach of warranty occurs when tender of delivery is made. c. A breach of a warranty of future performance of the goods occurs when the breach is or should have been discovered.***

(3) Saving Provision Allowing an Additional 6 Months for New Actions:

- ***a. If an action was commenced within the subsection (1) limitation but is then terminated leaving a remedy still available for the same breach, a new action may be commenced:***
  1. ***After the expiration of the time limited (as per 2-725(l)); but***
  2. ***Within 6 months after the termination of the first action***
- ***b. Exception - If the termination resulted from:***
  1. ***Voluntary discontinuance; or***
  2. ***Dismissal for failure or neglect to prosecute***

(4) This Section does not:

- ***a. Alter or modify the law on tolling of the Statute of Limitations***
- ***b. Apply to causes of action which accrued before this Act became effective***

TITLE 6

Commerce and Trade

SUBTITLE I

Uniform Commercial Code

ARTICLE 5 - LETTERS OF CREDIT

PART 1

Commerce and Trade

§ 5-101. Short title.

This Article may be cited as Uniform Commercial Code -- Letters of Credit. (5A Del. C. 1953, § 5-101; 55 Del. Laws, c. 349; 71 Del. Laws, c. 393, § 1.)

This Article may be cited as Uniform Commercial Code

§ 5-102. Definitions.

(a) In this Article:

(1) "Adviser" means a person who, at the request of the issuer, a confirmer, or another adviser, notifies or requests another adviser to notify the beneficiary that a letter of credit has been issued, confirmed, or amended.

(2) "Applicant" means a person at whose request or for whose account a letter of credit is issued. The term includes a person who requests an issuer to issue a letter of credit on behalf of another if the person making the request undertakes an obligation to reimburse the issuer.

(3) "Beneficiary" means a person who under the terms of a letter of credit is entitled to have its complying presentation honored. The term includes a person to whom drawing rights have been transferred under a transferable letter of credit.

(4) "Confirmer" means a nominated person who undertakes, at the request or with the consent of the issuer, to honor a presentation under a letter of credit issued by another.

(5) "Dishonor" of a letter of credit means failure timely to honor or to take an interim action, such as acceptance of a draft, that may be required by the letter of credit.

(6) "Document" means a draft or other demand, document of title, investment security, certificate, invoice, or other record, statement, or representation of fact, law, right, or opinion (i) which is presented in a written or other medium permitted by the letter of credit or, unless prohibited by the letter of credit, by the standard practice referred to in Section 5-108(e) and (ii) which is capable of being examined for compliance with the terms and conditions of the letter of credit. A document may not be oral.

(7) "Good faith" means honesty in fact in the conduct or transaction concerned.

(8) "Honor" of a letter of credit means performance of the issuer's undertaking in the letter of credit to pay or deliver an item of value. Unless the letter of credit otherwise provides, "honor" occurs

(i) upon payment,

(ii) if the letter of credit provides for acceptance, upon acceptance of a draft and, at maturity, its payment, or

(iii) if the letter of credit provides for incurring a deferred obligation, upon incurring the obligation and, at maturity, its performance.

(9) "Issuer" means a bank or other person that issues a letter of credit, but does not include an individual who makes an engagement for personal, family, or household purposes.

(10) "Letter of credit" means a definite undertaking that satisfies the requirements of Section 5-104 by an issuer to a beneficiary at the request or for the account of an applicant or, in the case of a financial institution, to itself or for its own account, to honor a documentary presentation by payment or delivery of an item of value.

(11) "Nominated person" means a person whom the issuer (i) designates or authorizes to pay, accept, negotiate, or otherwise give value under a letter of credit and (ii) undertakes by agreement or custom and practice to reimburse.

(12) "Presentation" means delivery of a document to an issuer or nominated person for honor or giving of value under a letter of credit.

(13) "Presenter" means a person making a presentation as or on behalf of a beneficiary or nominated person.

(14) "Record" means information that is inscribed on a tangible medium, or that is stored in an electronic or other medium and is retrievable in perceivable form.

(15) "Successor of a beneficiary" means a person who succeeds to substantially all of the rights of a beneficiary by operation of law, including a corporation with or into which the beneficiary has been merged or consolidated, an administrator, executor, personal representative, trustee in bankruptcy, debtor in possession, liquidator, and receiver.

(b) Definitions in other Articles applying to this Article and the Sections in which they appear are:

"Accept" or "Acceptance" Section 3-409

"Value" Sections 3-303, 4-211

(c) Article 1 contains certain additional general definitions and principles of construction and interpretation applicable throughout this Article. (5A Del. C. 1953, § 5-103; 55 Del. Laws, c. 349; 71 Del. Laws, c. 393, § 1.)

See above: Definitions

§ 5-103. Scope.

(a) This Article applies to letters of credit and to certain rights and obligations arising out of transactions involving letters of credit.

(b) The statement of a rule in this Article does not by itself require, imply, or negate application of the same or a different rule to a situation not provided for, or to a person not specified, in this Article.

(c) With the exception of this subsection, subsections (a) and (d), Sections 5-102(a)(9) and (10), 5-106(d), and 5-114(d), and except to the extent prohibited in Sections 1-102(3) and 5-117(d), the effect of this Article may be varied by agreement or by a provision stated or incorporated by reference in an undertaking. A term in an agreement or undertaking generally excusing liability or generally limiting remedies for failure to perform obligations is not sufficient to vary obligations prescribed by this Article.

(d) Rights and obligations of an issuer to a beneficiary or a nominated person under a letter of credit are independent of the existence, performance, or nonperformance of a contract or arrangement out of which the letter of credit arises or which underlies it, including contracts or arrangements between the issuer and the applicant and between the applicant and the beneficiary. (5A Del. C. 1953, § 5-102; 55 Del. Laws, c. 349; 71 Del. Laws, c. 393, § 1.)

See above.

§ 5-104. Formal requirements.

A letter of credit, confirmation, advice, transfer, amendment, or cancellation may be issued in any form that is a record and is authenticated (i) by a signature or (ii) in accordance with the agreement of the parties or the standard practice referred to in Section 5-108(e). (5A Del. C. 1953, § 5-104; 55 Del. Laws, c. 349; 71 Del. Laws, c. 393, § 1.)

A letter of credit, confirmation, advice, transfer, amendment, or cancellation may be issued in any form that is a record and is authenticated (i) by a signature or (ii) in accordance with the agreement of the parties or the standard practice referred to in Section 5-108(e).

§ 5-105. Consideration.

Consideration is not required to issue, amend, transfer, or cancel a letter of credit, advice, or confirmation. (5A Del. C. 1953, § 5-105; 55 Del. Laws, c. 349; 71 Del. Laws, c. 393, § 1.)

Consideration is not required to issue, amend, transfer, or cancel a letter of credit, advice, or confirmation.

§ 5-106. Issuance, amendment, cancellation, and duration.

(a) A letter of credit is issued and becomes enforceable according to its terms against the issuer when the issuer sends or otherwise transmits it to the person requested to advise or to the beneficiary. A letter of credit is revocable only if it so provides.

(b) After a letter of credit is issued, rights and obligations of a beneficiary, applicant, confirmer, and issuer are not affected by an amendment or cancellation to which that person has not consented except to the extent the letter of credit provides that it is revocable or that the issuer may amend or cancel the letter of credit without that consent.

(c) If there is no stated expiration date or other provision that determines its duration, a letter of credit expires one year after its stated date of issuance or, if none is stated, after the date on which it is issued.

(d) A letter of credit that states that it is perpetual expires five years after its stated date of issuance, or if none is stated, after the date on which it is issued. (5A Del. C. 1953, § 5-106; 55 Del. Laws, c. 349; 71 Del. Laws, c. 393, § 1.)

RULE §5-106. Issuance, amendment, cancellation, and duration.

(a) A letter of credit is issued and becomes enforceable according to its terms against the issuer when the issuer sends or otherwise transmits it to the person requested to advise or to the beneficiary. A letter of credit is revocable only if it so provides.

(b) After a letter of credit is issued, rights and obligations of a beneficiary, applicant, confirmer, and issuer are not affected by an amendment or cancellation to which that person has not consented except to the extent the letter of credit provides that it is revocable or that the issuer may amend or cancel the

letter of credit without that consent.

(c) If there is no stated expiration date or other provision that determines its duration, a letter of credit expires one year after its stated date of issuance or, if none is stated, after the date on which it is issued.

(d) A letter of credit that states that it is perpetual expires five years after its stated date of issuance, or if none is stated, after the date on which it is issued. (5A Del. C. 1953, § 5-106; 55 Del. Laws, c. 349; 71 Del. Laws, c. 393, § 1.)

§ 5-107. Confirmer, nominated person, and adviser.

(a) A confirmer is directly obligated on a letter of credit and has the rights and obligations of an issuer to the extent of its confirmation. The confirmer also has rights against and obligations to the issuer as if the issuer were an applicant and the confirmer had issued the letter of credit at the request and for the account of the issuer.

(b) A nominated person who is not a confirmer is not obligated to honor or otherwise give value for a presentation.

(c) A person requested to advise may decline to act as an adviser. An adviser that is not a confirmer is not obligated to honor or give value for a presentation. An adviser undertakes to the issuer and to the beneficiary accurately to advise the terms of the letter of credit, confirmation, amendment, or advice received by that person and undertakes to the beneficiary to check the apparent authenticity of the request to advise. Even if the advice is inaccurate, the letter of credit, confirmation, or amendment is enforceable as issued.

(d) A person who notifies a transferee beneficiary of the terms of a letter of credit, confirmation, amendment, or advice has the rights and obligations of an adviser under subsection (c). The terms in the notice to the transferee beneficiary may differ from the terms in any notice to the transferor beneficiary to the extent permitted by the letter of credit, confirmation, amendment, or advice received by the person who so notifies. (5A Del. C. 1953, § 5-107; 55 Del. Laws, c. 349; 71 Del. Laws, c. 393, § 1.)

RULE §5-107. Confirmer, nominated person, and adviser.

(a) A confirmer is directly obligated on a letter of credit and has the rights and obligations of an issuer to the extent of its confirmation. The confirmer also has rights against and obligations to the issuer as if the issuer were an applicant and the confirmer had issued the letter of credit at the request and for the account of the issuer.

(b) A nominated person who is not a confirmer is not obligated to honor or otherwise give value for a presentation.

(c) A person requested to advise may decline to act as an adviser. Even if the advice is inaccurate, the letter of credit, confirmation, or amendment is enforceable as issued.

(d) A person who notifies a transferee beneficiary of the terms of a letter of credit, confirmation, amendment, or advice has the rights and obligations of an adviser under subsection (c). The terms in the notice to the transferee beneficiary may differ from the terms in any notice to the transferor beneficiary to the extent permitted by the letter of credit, confirmation, amendment, or advice received by the person who so notifies.

§ 5-108. Issuer's rights and obligations.

(a) Except as otherwise provided in Section 5-109, an issuer shall honor a presentation that, as determined by the standard practice referred to in subsection (e), appears on its face strictly to comply with the terms and conditions of the letter of credit. Except as otherwise provided in Section 5-113 and unless otherwise agreed with the applicant, an issuer shall dishonor a presentation that does not appear so to comply.

(b) An issuer has a reasonable time after presentation, but not beyond the end of the seventh business day of the issuer after the day of its receipt of documents:

(1) to honor,

(2) if the letter of credit provides for honor to be completed more than seven business days after presentation, to accept a draft or incur a deferred obligation, or

(3) to give notice to the presenter of discrepancies in the presentation.

(c) Except as otherwise provided in subsection (d), an issuer is precluded from asserting as a basis for dishonor any discrepancy if timely notice is not given, or any discrepancy not stated in the notice if timely notice is given.

(d) Failure to give the notice specified in subsection (b) or to mention fraud, forgery, or expiration in the notice does not preclude the issuer from asserting as a basis for dishonor fraud or forgery as described in Section 5-109(a) or expiration of the letter of credit before presentation.

(e) An issuer shall observe standard practice of financial institutions that regularly issue letters of credit. Determination of the issuer's observance of the standard practice is a matter of interpretation for the court. The court shall offer the parties a reasonable opportunity to present evidence of the standard practice.

(f) An issuer is not responsible for:

(1) the performance or nonperformance of the underlying contract, arrangement, or transaction,

(2) an act or omission of others, or

(3) observance or knowledge of the usage of a particular trade other than the standard practice referred to in subsection (e).

(g) If an undertaking constituting a letter of credit under Section 5-102(a)(10) contains non-documentary conditions, an issuer shall disregard the non-documentary conditions and treat them as if they were not stated.

(h) An issuer that has dishonored a presentation shall return the documents or hold them at the disposal of, and send advice to that effect to, the presenter.

(i) An issuer that has honored a presentation as permitted or required by this Article:

(1) is entitled to be reimbursed by the applicant in immediately available funds not later than the date of its payment of funds;

(2) takes the documents free of claims of the beneficiary or presenter;

(3) is precluded from asserting a right of recourse on a draft under Sections 3-414 and 3-415;

(4) except as otherwise provided in Sections 5-110 and 5-117, is precluded from restitution of money paid or other value given by mistake to the extent the mistake concerns discrepancies in the documents or tender which are apparent on the face of the presentation; and

(5) is discharged to the extent of its performance under the letter of credit. (5A Del. C. 1953, § 5-109; 55 Del. Laws, c. 349; 71 Del. Laws, c. 393, § 1.)

RULE §5-108: Issuer's Rights and Obligations:

(a) Issuing Bank's Obligations:

- ***1) <u>When Issuer Must Honor:</u> An Issuer Bank shall honor a Presentation only if it appears to comply with the terms of the Letter of Credit (as determined by the "Standard Practice" referred to in §5-108(e)).***
- ***2) <u>When Issuer Does Not Have to Honor:</u>***
  <u>Fraud Exception</u> The Bank does not have to comply if there is evidence of Fraud (as per §5-109).
- ***3) <u>Non-Compliance:</u> An Issuer shall Dishonor a Presentation that does not comply with the Letter of Credit, unless:***
  - ***a) The Applicant otherwise directs the Issuer***
  - ***b) Otherwise provided where there is a Transfer by Operation of Law (as per §5-113).***

(b) Time Limits:

- ***1) <u>Time Limit:</u> An Issuer must honor, accept, or notify, by the earlier of***
  - ***i) A Reasonable Time***
  - ***ii) <u>7 Business Days</u> after receiving documents (upon Presentation)***
- ***2) <u>Application of Time Limit:</u> The above time limit applies to the following:***
  - ***i) <u>Honoring an L/C</u>***
  - ***ii) <u>Accepting a Draft,</u> (or incurring a "deferred obligation") - if the L/C provides for the L/C to be***

completed more than 7 Business Days after Presentation.

iii) Give Notice to the Presenter - of any discrepancies in the Presentation

(c) Failure to Give Notice of Discrepancies - If the Issuer fails to timely notify the Presenter of a discrepancy, the Issuer may not use such discrepancy as a basis for Dishonoring the L/C (except as provided in §5-108(d)).

(d) Failure to Give Notice of Fraud - Even if the Issuer fails to timely notify the Presenter of a discrepancy (as per §5-108(b)) or that there may be Fraud, Forgery, or that the L/C has expired, the Issuer may still assert Expiration or Fraud and Forgery (as per §5-109(a)) as a basis for dishonor.

(e) Issuer's Standard of Practice -

1. Standard of Care - An Issuer shall observe Standard Practice of Financial Institutions that regularly issue Letters of Credit.

2. Whether an Issuer has met this standard is an issued to be determined by the Court (and not a jury).

3. The court shall allow the parties a reasonable opportunity to present evidence of the "standard practice".

(f) Independent Significance: An Issuer is not responsible for:

(1) The Underlying Contract - the performance or nonperformance of the underlying contract

(2) An act or omission of others

(3) Trade Terms - Observance or knowledge of usage of a particular trade (unless it should know under "Standard Practice" as determined in §5-108(e) above)

(g) Non-documentary Conditions - The Issuer shall ignore any conditions in an Undertaking (constituting an LC under §5-102(a)(10)) which are Non-documentary conditions (ex: conditions to payment which are not

evidenced by documents to be presented to Issuer).

(h) Dishonor - If an Issuer has Dishonored an L/C, it shall do the following:
- ***1) Return the documents; or***
- ***2) Both:***
  - ***a) Hold the documents (at the disposal of the Presenter); and***
  - ***b) Send the Presenter notice that such documents are being held by the Issuer***

(i) Issuer's Rights - After appropriately honoring an L/C, the Issuer will have the following rights:

(1) <u>Reimbursement</u> - the Issuer is entitled to Reimbursement by the Applicant no later than the <u>date of Issuer's Payment</u> of the L/C.

(2) <u>Free & Clear Documents</u> - the Issuer takes the documents free any claims from the:
- ***i) Beneficiary***
- ***ii) Presenter***

(3) <u>Limited Right of Recourse</u> - the Issuer may not assert a right of recourse against the Drawer or Indorser of a Draft (under §3-414 or §3-415)

(4) <u>No Restitution for Mistake</u> - the Issuer will be precluded from obtaining restitution for money paid (or value given) by Mistake:
- ***a) To the Extent the Mistake concerns***
  - ***i) Discrepancies in the documents (which the Issuer should have spotted)***
  - ***ii) Discrepancies in Tender (which was apparent on the face of the documents presented)***
- ***b) Unless otherwise provided for in Warranties (§5-110) or with Subrogation Rights (arising under §5-177).***

(5) <u>Discharge</u> - The Issuer will be discharged of its

obligations to the Applicant, to the extent of its performance under the L/C unless the Issuer honored a presentation with a forged signature of a Beneficiary required to sign a presented document.

§ 5-109. Fraud and forgery.

(a) If a presentation is made that appears on its face strictly to comply with the terms and conditions of the letter of credit, but a required document is forged or materially fraudulent, or honor of the presentation would facilitate a material fraud by the beneficiary on the issuer or applicant:

(1) the issuer shall honor the presentation, if honor is demanded by (i) a nominated person who has given value in good faith and without notice of forgery or material fraud, (ii) a confirmer who has honored its confirmation in good faith, (iii) a holder in due course of a draft drawn under the letter of credit which was taken after acceptance by the issuer or nominated person, or (iv) an assignee of the issuer's or nominated person's deferred obligation that was taken for value and without notice of forgery or material fraud after the obligation was incurred by the issuer or nominated person; and

(2) the issuer, acting in good faith, may honor or dishonor the presentation in any other case.

(b) If an applicant claims that a required document is forged or materially fraudulent or that honor of the presentation would facilitate a material fraud by the beneficiary on the issuer or applicant, a court of competent jurisdiction may temporarily or permanently enjoin the issuer from honoring a presentation or grant similar relief against the issuer or other persons only if the court finds that:

(1) the relief is not prohibited under the law applicable to an accepted draft or deferred obligation incurred by the issuer;

(2) a beneficiary, issuer, or nominated person who may be adversely affected is adequately protected against loss that it may suffer because the relief is granted;

(3) all of the conditions to entitle a person to the relief under the law of this State have been met; and

(4) on the basis of the information submitted to the court, the applicant is more likely than not to succeed under its claim of forgery or material fraud and the person demanding honor does not qualify for protection under subsection (a)(1). (71 Del. Laws, c. 393, § 1.)

RULE §5-109: Fraud or Forgery:

(a) Fraudulent Presentation -

i) Scope: The following rules apply if

a) a document that is presented appears to comply, on its face, to the L/C; and

b) Either:

1) A required document is Forged or Materially Fraudulent; or

2) Honor of the Presentation would facilitate a Material Fraud by the Beneficiary (hurting the Issuer or Applicant):

ii) Rules of Honoring with Forged/Fraudulent Documents:

(1) Protected Beneficiaries: The Issuer shall Honor the presentation if Honor is demanded by:

or (i) A Nominated Person if:

a. It was given Value; and b. In Good Faith; and

C. Without Notice of Forgery

or (ii) A Confirmer - who has honored its confirmation in Good Faith

or (iii) A Holder in Due Course if:

1. It is the Holder of a Draft drawn under the L/C; and

2. The draft was taken After Acceptance by the Issuer (or Nominated Party)

or (iv) An Assignee of the Issuer's or Nominated Person's Deferred Obligation (as per §5-108(b)(2)) if:

1. It was taken for Value; and

2. Without Notice of Forgery; and

3. After the Obligation was incurred by the Issuer (or Nominated Person)
and (2) Issuer's Discretion- the Issuer may honor or dishonor the presentation while acting in Good Faith.

(b) Injunctions:
The court may not temporarily or permanently enjoin the Issuer from Honoring a Presentation (or it may grant similar relief against the Issuer or other persons) unless the court finds that:
(1) Applicable Law Allows Relief: The relief is not prohibited under the law applicable to the Accepted Draft or Deferred Obligation; and
(2) Adequate Protection: The Beneficiary, Issuer, or Nominated Person (who may be adversely affected by the injunction) is adequately protected against any loss it may incur as a result of the relief; and
(3) State Law Satisfied: All the requirements for the particular relief under state law have been met; and
(4) Applicant Likely to Succeed:
1. The Applicant is more likely than not to succeed under its claim of forgery or material Fraud; and
2. The person demanding honor doesn't qualify for protection under §5-109(a)(1).
and (5) An Applicant claims that a Required Document:
a. Is Forged; or
b. Is Materially Forged; or
c. Would facilitate a Material Fraud by the Beneficiary (hurting the Issuer or Applicant).

§ 5-110. Warranties.

(a) If its presentation is honored, the beneficiary warrants:

(1) to the issuer, any other person to whom presentation is made, and the applicant that there is no fraud or forgery of the kind described in Section 5-109(a); and

(2) to the applicant that the drawing does not violate any agreement between the applicant and beneficiary or any other agreement intended by them to be augmented by the letter of credit.

(b) The warranties in subsection (a) are in addition to warranties arising under Article 3, 4, 7, and 8 because of the presentation or transfer of documents covered by any of those Articles. (5A Del. C. 1953, § 5-111; 55 Del. Laws, c. 349; 71 Del. Laws, c. 393, § 1.)

RULE § 5-110. Warranties.

(a) If its presentation is honored, the beneficiary warrants:

(1) to the issuer, any other person to whom presentation is made, and the applicant that there is no fraud or forgery of the kind described in Section 5-109(a); and

(2) to the applicant that the drawing does not violate any agreement between the applicant and beneficiary or any other agreement intended by them to be augmented by the letter of credit.

(b) The warranties in subsection (a) are in addition to warranties arising under Article 3, 4, 7, and 8 because of the presentation or transfer of documents covered by any of those Articles.

§ 5-111. Remedies.

(a) If an issuer wrongfully dishonors or repudiates its obligation to pay money under a letter of credit before presentation, the beneficiary, successor, or nominated person presenting on its own behalf may recover from the issuer the amount that is the subject of the dishonor or repudiation. If the issuer's obligation under the letter of credit is not for the payment of money, the claimant may obtain specific performance or, at the claimant's election, recover an amount equal to the value of performance from the issuer. In either case, the claimant may also recover incidental but not consequential damages. The claimant is not obligated to take action to avoid damages that might be due from the issuer under this subsection. If, although not obligated to do so, the claimant avoids damages, the claimant's recovery from the issuer must be reduced by the amount of damages avoided. The issuer has the burden of proving the amount of damages avoided. In the case of repudiation the claimant need not present any document.

(b) If an issuer wrongfully dishonors a draft or demand presented under a letter of credit or honors a draft or demand in breach of its obligation to the applicant, the applicant may recover damages resulting from the breach, including incidental but not consequential damages, less any amount saved as a result of the breach.

(c) If an adviser or nominated person other than a confirmer breaches an obligation under this Article or an issuer breaches an obligation not covered in subsection (a) or (b), a person to whom the obligation is owed may recover damages resulting from the breach, including incidental but not consequential damages, less any amount saved as a result of the breach. To the extent of the confirmation, a confirmer has the liability of an issuer specified in this subsection and subsections (a) and (b).

(d) An issuer, nominated person, or adviser who is found liable under subsection (a), (b), or (c) shall pay interest on the amount owed thereunder from the date of wrongful dishonor or other appropriate date.

(e) Reasonable attorney's fees and other expenses of litigation must be awarded to the prevailing party in an action in which a remedy is sought under this article.

(f) Damages that would otherwise be payable by a party for breach of an obligation under this article may be liquidated by agreement or undertaking, but only in an amount or by a formula that is reasonable in light of the harm anticipated. (5A Del. C. 1953, § 5-115; 55 Del. Laws, c. 349; 71 Del. Laws, c. 393, § 1.)

See above.

§ 5-112. Transfer of letter of credit.

(a) Except as otherwise provided in Section 5-113, unless a letter of credit provides that it is transferable, the right of a beneficiary to draw or otherwise demand performance under a letter of credit may not be transferred.

(b) Even if a letter of credit provides that it is transferable, the issuer may refuse to recognize or carry out a transfer if:

(1) the transfer would violate applicable law; or

(2) the transferor or transferee has failed to comply with any requirement stated in the letter of credit or any other requirement relating to transfer imposed by the issuer which is within the standard practice referred to in Section 5-108(e) or is otherwise reasonable under the circumstances. (5A Del. C. 1953, § 5-116; 55 Del. Laws, c. 349; 64 Del. Laws, c. 152, § 5; 71 Del. Laws, c. 393, § 1.)

RULE §5-112. Transfer of letter of credit.

(a) Except as otherwise provided in Section 5-113, unless a letter of credit provides that it is transferable, the right of a beneficiary to draw or otherwise demand performance under a letter of credit may not be transferred.

(b) Even if a letter of credit provides that it is transferable, the issuer may refuse to recognize or carry out a transfer if:

(1) the transfer would violate applicable law; or
(2) the transferor or transferee has failed to comply with any requirement stated in the letter of credit or any other requirement relating to transfer imposed by the issuer which is within the standard practice referred to in Section 5-108(e) or is otherwise reasonable under the circumstances.

§ 5-113. Transfer by operation of law.

(a) A successor of a beneficiary may consent to amendments, sign and present documents, and receive payment or other items of value in the name of the beneficiary without disclosing its status as a successor.

(b) A successor of a beneficiary may consent to amendments, sign and present documents, and receive payment or other items of value in its own name as the disclosed successor of the beneficiary. Except as otherwise provided in subsection (e), an issuer shall recognize a disclosed successor of a beneficiary as beneficiary in full substitution for its predecessor upon compliance with the requirements for recognition by the issuer of a transfer of drawing rights by operation of law under the standard practice referred to in Section 5-108(e) or, in the absence of such a practice, compliance with other reasonable procedures sufficient to protect the issuer.

(c) An issuer is not obliged to determine whether a purported successor is a successor of a beneficiary or whether the signature of a purported successor is genuine or authorized.

(d) Honor of a purported successor's apparently complying presentation under subsection (a) or (b) has the consequences specified in Section 5-108(i) even if the purported successor is not the successor of a beneficiary. Documents signed in the name of the beneficiary or of a disclosed successor by a person who is neither the beneficiary nor the successor of the beneficiary are forged documents for the purposes of Section 5-109.

(e) An issuer whose rights of reimbursement are not covered by subsection (d) or substantially similar law and any confirmer or nominated person may decline to recognize a presentation under subsection (b).

(f) A beneficiary whose name is changed after the issuance of a letter of credit has the same rights and obligations as a successor of a beneficiary under this Section. (71 Del. Laws, c. 393, § 1.)

RULE §5-113. Transfer by operation of law.

(a) A successor of a beneficiary may consent to amendments, sign and present documents, and receive payment or other items of value in the name of the beneficiary without disclosing its status as a successor.

(b) A successor of a beneficiary may consent to amendments, sign and present documents, and receive payment or other items of value in its own name as the disclosed successor of the beneficiary. Except as otherwise provided in subsection (e), an issuer shall recognize a disclosed successor of a beneficiary as beneficiary in full substitution for its predecessor upon compliance with the requirements for recognition by the issuer of a transfer of drawing rights by operation of law under the standard practice referred to in Section 5-108(e) or, in the absence of such a practice, compliance with other reasonable procedures

sufficient to protect the issuer.

(c) An issuer is not obliged to determine whether a purported successor is a successor of a beneficiary or whether the signature of a purported successor is genuine or authorized.

(d) Honor of a purported successor's apparently complying presentation under subsection (a) or (b) has the consequences specified in Section 5-108(i) even if the purported successor is not the successor of a beneficiary. Documents signed in the name of the beneficiary or of a disclosed successor by a person who is neither the beneficiary nor the successor of the beneficiary are forged documents for the purposes of Section 5-109.

(e) An issuer whose rights of reimbursement are not covered by subsection (d) or substantially similar law and any confirmer or nominated person may decline to recognize a presentation under subsection (b).

(f) A beneficiary whose name is changed after the issuance of a letter of credit has the same rights and obligations as a successor of a beneficiary under this Section.

§ 5-114. Assignment of proceeds.

(a) In this Section, "proceeds of a letter of credit" means the cash, check, accepted draft, or other item of value paid or delivered upon honor or giving of value by the issuer or any nominated person under the letter of credit. The term does not include a beneficiary's drawing rights or documents presented by the beneficiary.

(b) A beneficiary may assign its right to part or all of the proceeds of a letter of credit. The beneficiary may do so before presentation as a present assignment of its right to receive proceeds contingent upon its compliance with the terms and conditions of the letter of credit.

(c) An issuer or nominated person need not recognize an assignment of proceeds of a letter of credit until it consents to the assignment.

(d) An issuer or nominated person has no obligation to give or withhold its consent to an assignment of proceeds of a letter of credit, but consent may not be unreasonably withheld if the assignee possesses and exhibits the letter of credit and presentation of the letter of credit is a condition to honor.

(e) Rights of a transferee beneficiary or nominated person are independent of the beneficiary's assignment of the proceeds of a letter of credit and are superior to the assignee's right to the proceeds.

(f) Neither the rights recognized by this Section between an assignee and an issuer, transferee beneficiary, or nominated person nor the issuer's or nominated person's payment of proceeds to an assignee or a third person affect the rights between the assignee and any person other than the issuer, transferee beneficiary, or nominated person. The mode of creating and perfecting a security interest in or granting an assignment of a beneficiary's rights to proceeds is governed by Article 9 or other law. Against persons other than the issuer, transferee beneficiary, or nominated person, the rights and obligations arising upon the creation of a security interest or other assignment of a beneficiary's right to proceeds and its perfection are governed by Article 9 or other law. (71 Del. Laws, c. 393, § 1.)

RULE §5-114. Assignment of proceeds.

(a) In this Section, "proceeds of a letter of credit" means the cash, check, accepted draft, or other item of value paid or delivered upon honor or giving of value by the issuer or any nominated person under the letter of credit. The term does not include a beneficiary's drawing rights or documents presented by the beneficiary.

(b) A beneficiary may assign its right to part or all of the proceeds of a letter of credit. The beneficiary may do so before presentation as a present assignment of its right to receive proceeds contingent upon its compliance with the terms and conditions of the letter of credit.

(c) An issuer or nominated person need not recognize an assignment of proceeds of a letter of credit until it consents

to the assignment.

(d) An issuer or nominated person has no obligation to give or withhold its consent to an assignment of proceeds of a letter of credit, but consent may not be unreasonably withheld if the assignee possesses and exhibits the letter of credit and presentation of the letter of credit is a condition to honor.

(e) Rights of a transferee beneficiary or nominated person are independent of the beneficiary's assignment of the proceeds of a letter of credit and are superior to the assignee's right to the proceeds.

(f) Neither the rights recognized by this Section between an assignee and an issuer, transferee beneficiary, or nominated person nor the issuer's or nominated person's payment of proceeds to an assignee or a third person affect the rights between the assignee and any person other than the issuer, transferee beneficiary, or nominated person. The mode of creating and perfecting a security interest in or granting an assignment of a beneficiary's rights to proceeds is governed by Article 9 or other law. Against persons other than the issuer, transferee beneficiary, or nominated person, the rights and obligations arising upon the creation of a security interest or other assignment of a beneficiary's right to proceeds and its perfection are governed by Article 9 or other law.

§ 5-115. Statute of limitations.

An action to enforce a right or obligation arising under this Article must be commenced within one year after the expiration date of the relevant letter of credit or one year after the cause of action accrues, whichever occurs later. A cause of action accrues when the breach occurs, regardless of the aggrieved party's lack of knowledge of the breach. (71 Del. Laws, c. 393, § 1.)

RULE §5-115. Statute of limitations.

An action to enforce a right or obligation arising under this Article must be commenced within one year after the expiration date of the relevant letter of credit or one year after the cause of action accrues, whichever occurs later. A cause of action accrues when the breach occurs, regardless of the aggrieved party's lack of knowledge of the breach.

§ 5-116. Choice of law and forum.

(a) The liability of an issuer, nominated person, or adviser for action or omission is governed by the law of the jurisdiction chosen by an agreement in the form of a record signed or otherwise authenticated by the affected parties in the manner provided in Section 5-104 or by a provision in the person's letter of credit, confirmation, or other undertaking. The jurisdiction whose law is chosen need not bear any relation to the transaction.

(b) Unless subsection (a) applies, the liability of an issuer, nominated person, or adviser for action or omission is governed by the law of the jurisdiction in which the person is located. The person is considered to be located at the address indicated in the person's undertaking. If more than one address is indicated, the person is considered to be located at the address from which the person's undertaking was issued. For the purpose of jurisdiction, choice of law, and recognition of interbranch letters of credit, but not enforcement of a judgment, all branches of a bank are considered separate juridical entities and a bank is considered to be located at the place where its relevant branch is considered to be located under this subsection.

(c) Except as otherwise provided in this subsection, the liability of an issuer, nominated person, or adviser is governed by any rules of custom or practice, such as the Uniform Customs and Practice for Documentary Credits, to which the letter of credit, confirmation, or other undertaking is expressly made subject. If (i) this Article would govern the liability of an issuer, nominated person, or adviser under subsection (a) or (b), (ii) the relevant undertaking incorporates rules of custom or practice, and (iii) there is conflict between this Article and those rules as applied to that undertaking, those rules govern except to the extent of any conflict with the non-variable provisions specified in Section 5-103(c).

(d) If there is conflict between this Article and Article 3, 4, 4A, or 9, this Article governs.

(e) The forum for settling disputes arising out of an undertaking within this Article may be chosen in the manner and with the binding effect that governing law may be chosen in accordance with subsection (a). (71 Del. Laws, c. 393, § 1.)

See above.

§ 5-117. Subrogation of issuer, applicant, and nominated person.

(a) An issuer that honors a beneficiary's presentation is subrogated to the rights of the beneficiary to the same extent as if the issuer were a secondary obligor of the underlying obligation owed to the beneficiary and of the applicant to the same extent as if the issuer were the secondary obligor of the underlying obligation owed to the applicant.

(b) An applicant that reimburses an issuer is subrogated to the rights of the issuer against any beneficiary, presenter, or nominated person to the same extent as if the applicant were the secondary obligor of the obligations owed to the issuer and has the rights of subrogation of the issuer to the rights of the beneficiary stated in subsection (a).

(c) A nominated person who pays or gives value against a draft or demand presented under a letter of credit is subrogated to the rights of:

(1) the issuer against the applicant to the same extent as if the nominated person were a secondary obligor of the obligation owed to the issuer by the applicant;

(2) the beneficiary to the same extent as if the nominated person were a secondary obligor of the underlying obligation owed to the beneficiary; and

(3) the applicant to same extent as if the nominated person were a secondary obligor of the underlying obligation owed to the applicant.

(d) Notwithstanding any agreement or term to the contrary, the rights of subrogation stated in subsections (a) and (b) do not arise until the issuer honors the letter of credit or otherwise pays and the rights in subsection (c) do not arise until the nominated person pays or otherwise gives value. Until then, the issuer, nominated person, and the applicant do not derive under this Section present or prospective rights forming the basis of a claim, defense, or excuse. (71 Del. Laws, c. 393, § 1.)

See above.

§ 5-118. Security interest of issuer or nominated person.

(a) An issuer or nominated person has a security interest in a document presented under a letter of credit to the extent that the issuer or nominated person honors or gives value for the presentation.

(b) So long as and to the extent that an issuer or nominated person has not been reimbursed or has not otherwise recovered the value given with respect to a security interest in a document under subsection (a), the security interest continues and is subject to Article 9, but:

(1) a security agreement is not necessary to make the security interest enforceable under Section 9-203(b)(3);

(2) if the document is presented in a medium other than a written or other tangible medium, the security interest is perfected; and

(3) if the document is presented in a written or other tangible medium and is not a certificated security, chattel paper, a document of title, an instrument, or a letter of credit, the security interest is perfected and has priority over a conflicting security interest in the document so long as the debtor does not have possession of the document. (72 Del. Laws, c. 401, § 16.)

RULE §5-118. Security interest of issuer or nominated person.

(a) An issuer or nominated person has a security interest in a document presented under a letter of credit to the extent that the issuer or nominated person honors or gives value for the presentation.

(b) So long as and to the extent that an issuer or nominated person has not been reimbursed or has not otherwise recovered the value given with respect to a security interest in a document under subsection (a), the security interest continues and is subject to Article 9, but:

(1) a security agreement is not necessary to make the security interest enforceable under Section 9-203(b)(3);

(2) if the document is presented in a medium other than a written or other tangible medium, the security interest is perfected; and

(3) if the document is presented in a written or other tangible medium and is not a certificated security, chattel paper, a document of title, an instrument, or a letter of credit, the security interest is perfected and has priority over a conflicting security interest in the document so long as the debtor does not have possession of the document.

TITLE 6

Commerce and Trade

SUBTITLE I

Uniform Commercial Code

ARTICLE 7 - WAREHOUSE RECEIPTS, BILLS OF LADING AND OTHER DOCUMENTS OF TITLE

PART 1

General

§ 7-101. Short title.

This Article shall be known and may be cited as Uniform Commercial Code -- Documents of Title. (5A Del. C. 1953, § 7-101; 55 Del. Laws, c. 349.)

This Article shall be known and may be cited as Uniform Commercial Code -- Documents of Title.

§ 7-102. Definitions and index of definitions.

(1) In this Article, unless the context otherwise requires:

(a) "Bailee" means the person who by a warehouse receipt, bill of lading or other document of title acknowledges possession of goods and contracts to deliver them.

(b) "Consignee" means the person named in a bill to whom or to whose order the bill promises delivery.

(c) "Consignor" means the person named in a bill as the person from whom the goods have been received for shipment.

(d) "Delivery order" means a written order to deliver goods directed to a warehouseman, carrier or other person who in the ordinary course of business issues warehouse receipts or bills of lading.

(e) "Document" means document of title as defined in the general definitions in Article 1 (Section 1-201).

(f) "Goods" means all things which are treated as movable for the purpose of a contract of storage or transportation.

(g) "Issuer" means a bailee who issues a document except that in relation to an unaccepted delivery order it means the person who orders the possessor of goods to deliver. Issuer includes any person for whom an agent or employee purports to act in issuing a document if the agent or employee has real or apparent authority to issue documents, notwithstanding that the issuer received no goods or that the goods were misdescribed or that in any other respect the agent or employee violated his instructions.

(h) "Warehouseman" is a person engaged in the business of storing goods for hire.

(2) Other definitions applying to this Article or to specified Parts thereof, and the sections in which they appear are:

"Duly negotiate". Section 7-501.

"Person entitled under the document". Section 7-403(4).

(3) Definitions in other Articles applying to this Article and the sections in which they appear are:

"Contract for sale". Section 2-106.

"Overseas". Section 2-323.

"Receipt" of goods. Section 2-103.

(4) In addition Article 1 contains general definitions and principles of construction and interpretation applicable throughout this Article. (5A Del. C. 1953, § 7-102; 55 Del. Laws, c. 349.)

Definitions – See above

§ 7-103. Relation of Article to treaty, statute, tariff, classification or regulation.

To the extent that any treaty or statute of the United States, regulatory statute of this State or tariff, classification or regulation filed or issued pursuant thereto is applicable, this Article is subject thereto. (5A Del. C. 1953, § 7-103; 55 Del. Laws, c. 349.)

RULE §7-103. Relation of Article to treaty, statute, tariff, classification or regulation.

To the extent that any treaty or statute of the United States, regulatory statute of this State or tariff, classification or regulation filed or issued pursuant thereto is applicable, this Article is subject thereto.

§ 7-104. Negotiable and non-negotiable warehouse receipt, bill of lading or other document of title.

(1) A warehouse receipt, bill of lading or other document of title is negotiable

(a) if by its terms the goods are to be delivered to bearer or to the order of a named person; or

(b) where recognized in overseas trade, if it runs to a named person or assigns.

(2) Any other document is non-negotiable. A bill of lading in which it is stated that the goods are consigned to a named person is not made negotiable by a provision that the goods are to be delivered only against a written order signed by the same or another named person. (5A Del. C. 1953, § 7-104; 55 Del. Laws, c. 349.)

RULE §7-104. Negotiable and non-negotiable warehouse receipt, bill of lading or other document of title.

(1) A warehouse receipt, bill of lading or other document of title is negotiable
(a) if by its terms the goods are to be delivered to bearer or to the order of a named person; or
(b) where recognized in overseas trade, if it runs to a named person or assigns.
(2) Any other document is non-negotiable. A bill of lading in which it is stated that the goods are consigned to a named person is not made negotiable by a provision that the goods are to be delivered only against a written order signed by the same or another named person

§ 7-105. Construction against negative implication.

The omission from either Part 2 or Part 3 of this Article of a provision corresponding to a provision made in the other part does not imply that a corresponding rule of law is not applicable. (5A Del. C. 1953, § 7-105; 55 Del. Laws, c. 349.)

RULE §7-105. Construction against negative implication.

The omission from either Part 2 or Part 3 of this Article of a provision corresponding to a provision made in the other part does not imply that a corresponding rule of law is not applicable.

TITLE 6

Commerce and Trade

SUBTITLE I

Uniform Commercial Code

ARTICLE 7 - WAREHOUSE RECEIPTS, BILLS OF LADING AND OTHER DOCUMENTS OF TITLE

PART 5

Warehouse Receipts and Bills of Lading: Negotiation and Transfer

§ 7-501. Form of negotiation and requirements of "due negotiation."

(1) A negotiable document of title running to the order of a named person is negotiated by his indorsement and delivery. After his indorsement in blank or to bearer any person can negotiate it by delivery alone.

(2)(a) A negotiable document of title is also negotiated by delivery alone when by its original terms it runs to bearer.

(b) When a document running to the order of a named person is delivered to him the effect is the same as if the document had been negotiated.

(3) Negotiation of a negotiable document of title after it has been indorsed to a specified person requires indorsement by the special indorsee as well as delivery.

(4) A negotiable document of title is "duly negotiated" when it is negotiated in the manner stated in this section to a holder who purchases it in good faith without notice of any defense against or claim to it on the part of any person and for value, unless it is established that the negotiation is not in the regular course of business or financing or involves receiving the document in settlement or payment of a money obligation.

(5) Indorsement of a non-negotiable document neither makes it negotiable nor adds to the transferee's rights.

(6) The naming in a negotiable bill of a person to be notified of the arrival of the goods does not limit the negotiability of the bill nor constitute notice to a purchaser

thereof of any interest of such person in the goods. (5A Del. C. 1953, § 7-501; 55 Del. Laws, c. 349.)

RULE §7-501: Due Negotiation:

(1) Manner of Negotiation:

a) Named Person: A Negotiable Document of Title "running" to the order of a named person, can be negotiated only if:

(a) Indorsement - The identified person in the document Indoreses it; and

(b) Deliver - The document is delivered into the possession of the holder

b) Bearer: If the instrument is indorsed in blank (i.e. "to Bearer or has a "blank indorsement"), it can be negotiated by delivery alone.

(2) Delivery as Negotiation:

(a) A Negotiable Document of Title may also negotiated by Delivery alone if it "runs" to bearer (by its original terms). (b) A Document of Title will be considered as if it had been negotiated if it is delivered to the identified person.

(3) Special Indorsement: If a negotiable DOT has been indorsed to an identified person, the special indorsee must Indorse and Deliver it to negotiate it.

(4) "Due Negotiation": Requirements for a Negotiable Document of Title to be "duly negotiated"

a) It is Negotiated (in the manner stated above in this section) to a Holder (as per §l-201(20)); and

b) The Holder takes by Purchase (as per §l-201(32)); and

c) It is Purchased:

1. In Good Faith (as per §1-201(19)); and

2. Without any Notice of another person's claims or defenses against the document; and

3. For Value (as per §l-201(44)); and

4. In the <u>Regular Course of Business or financing</u> (i.e., from a merchant); and

d) It does NOT involve receiving the document in settlement or payment of a money obligation.

(5) Non-Negotiable Documents: Indorsement of a Non-Negotiable Document neither makes it negotiable nor adds to the transferee's rights

(6) Naming Person to Notify upon Arrival: The naming of a person (in a negotiable DOT) to be notified when goods (represented by the DOT) arrive <u>does not:</u>

a) Limit the negotiability of the bill; nor

b) Constitute notice to a purchaser of the bill the named person has any interest in the goods.

§ 7-502. Rights acquired by due negotiation.

(1) Subject to the following section and to the provisions of Section 7-205 on fungible goods, a holder to whom a negotiable document of title has been duly negotiated acquires thereby:

(a) title to the document;

(b) title to the goods;

(c) all rights accruing under the law of agency or estoppel, including rights to goods delivered to the bailee after the document was issued; and

(d) the direct obligation of the issuer to hold or deliver the goods according to the terms of the document free of any defense or claim by him except those arising under the terms of the document or under this Article. In the case of a delivery order the bailee's obligation accrues only upon acceptance and the obligation acquired by the holder is that the issuer and any indorser will procure the acceptance of the bailee.

(2) Subject to the following section, title and rights so acquired are not defeated by any stoppage of the goods represented by the document or by surrender of such goods by the bailee, and are not impaired even though the negotiation or any prior negotiation constituted a breach of duty or even though any person has been deprived of possession of the document by misrepresentation, fraud, accident, mistake, duress, loss, theft or conversion, or even though a previous sale or other transfer of the goods or document has been made to a third person. (5A Del. C. 1953, § 7-502; 55 Del. Laws, c. 349.)

RULE §7-502: Rights Acquired by Due Negotiation:

(1) Rights by Due negotiation: A person acquires the following rights if a Negotiable Document has been Duly Negotiated to him (subject to §7-205 and §2-703):

- ***(a) Title to the Documents; and***
- ***(b) Title to the Goods; and***
- ***(c) All rights accruing under the law of agency and estoppel (including rights to goods delivered to the bailee after the document was issued)***

and (d)

1. ***The Direct Obligation of the Issuer to Hold or Deliver the Goods according to the terms of the Document FREE of any defense or claim by the issuer (except those arising under the terms of the Document or Under Article 7)***
2. ***Delivery Order Cases: The Bailee's Obligation accrues only when***
   - ***a) The Bailee accepts its obligation; and***
   - ***b) The obligation acquired by the holder is that the Issuer (and any indorser) will procure the acceptance of the Bailee***

(2) Title and Rights (subject to §7-503)

- ***a) Title and rights acquired by negotiation will not be defeated by***
  - ***1) Any stoppage (of the goods represented by the document); or***
  - ***2) By surrender of the goods by the Bailee***
- ***b) Title and rights acquired by negotiation will not be impaired, even if***
  - ***1) Negotiation (or any prior negotiation) constituted a breach of duty***
  - ***2) Any person has been deprived of possession of the document by:***
    - ***a) Misrepresentation or b) Fraud; or***
    - ***c) Accident; or***

d) Mistake; or
e) Duress; or
f) Loss; or
g) Theft ;or
h) Conversion

3) A Previous sale (or other transfer of the goods or document) has made a third person.

§ 7-503. Document of title to goods defeated in certain cases.

(1) A document of title confers no right in goods against a person who before issuance of the document had a legal interest or a perfected security interest in them and who neither

(a) delivered or entrusted them or any document of title covering them to the bailor or his nominee with actual or apparent authority to ship, store or sell or with power to obtain delivery under this Article (Section 7-403) or with power of disposition under this subtitle (Sections 2-403 and 9-320) or other statute or rule of law; nor

(b) acquiesced in the procurement by the bailor or his nominee of any document of title.

(2) Title to goods based upon an unaccepted delivery order is subject to the rights of anyone to whom a negotiable warehouse receipt or bill of lading covering the goods has been duly negotiated. Such a title may be defeated under the next section to the same extent as the rights of the issuer or a transferee from the issuer.

(3) Title to goods based upon a bill of lading issued to a freight forwarder is subject to the rights of anyone to whom a bill issued by the freight forwarded is duly negotiated; but delivery by the carrier in accordance with Part 4 of this Article pursuant to its own bill of lading discharges the carrier's obligation to deliver. (5A Del. C. 1953, § 7-503; 55 Del. Laws, c. 349; 72 Del. Laws, c. 401, § 17.)

RULE §7-503: Defeated Documents of Title:

(1) <u>Interests before Issuance:</u> A DOT confers no right in goods against a person who:
(a) Didn't delivered or entrust such goods (or DOT covering them) to a merchant (as per §2-403); and

(b) Didn't acquiesce title in the procurement by the Bailor (or his nominee) of any DOT; and

(c) Had a legal or perfected S/I in the goods before the Document was issued

(2) <u>Unaccented Delivery Orders:</u>

(a) Title to goods based upon an unaccepted delivery order is subject to the rights of anyone to whom a Negotiable warehouse receipt or BOL (covering such goods) has been Duly Negotiated.

(b) Such a title may be defeated under §7-504 to the same extent as the rights of the Issuer or a Transferee from the Issuer.

(3) <u>BOL issued to a Freight Forwarder</u>

(a) Title to goods based on a BOL issued to a Freight Forwarder is subject to the rights of anyone to whom a bill issued to the Freight Forwarder is <u>Duly Negotiated</u>

(b) Delivery by the carrier (in accordance with Part 4 of Article 7) pursuant to its own BOL, discharges the carrier's obligation to deliver.

§ 7-504. Rights acquired in the absence of due negotiation; effect of diversion; seller's stoppage of delivery.

(1) A transferee of a document, whether negotiable or non-negotiable, to whom the document has been delivered but not duly negotiated, acquires the title and rights which his transferor had or had actual authority to convey.

(2) In the case of a non-negotiable document, until but not after the bailee receives notification of the transfer, the rights of the transferee may be defeated

(a) by those creditors of the transferor who could treat the sale as void under Section 2-402; or

(b) by a buyer from the transferor in ordinary course of business if the bailee has delivered the goods to the buyer or received notification of his rights; or

(c) as against the bailee by good faith dealings of the bailee with the transferor.

(3) A diversion or other change of shipping instructions by the consignor in a non-negotiable bill of lading which causes the bailee not to deliver to the consignee defeats the consignee's title to the goods if they have been delivered to a buyer in ordinary course of business and in any event defeats the consignee's rights against the bailee.

(4) Delivery pursuant to a non-negotiable document may be stopped by a seller under Section 2-705, and subject to the requirement of due notification there provided. A bailee honoring the seller's instructions is entitled to be indemnified by the seller against any resulting loss or expense. (5A Del. C. 1953, § 7-504; 55 Del. Laws, c. 349.)

RULE §7-504. Rights acquired in the absence of due negotiation; effect of diversion; seller's stoppage of delivery.

(1) A transferee of a document, whether negotiable or non-negotiable, to whom the document has been delivered but not duly negotiated, acquires the title and rights which his transferor had or had actual authority to convey.

(2) In the case of a non-negotiable document, until but not after the bailee receives notification of the transfer, the rights of the transferee may be defeated

(a) by those creditors of the transferor who could treat the sale as void under Section 2-402; or

(b) by a buyer from the transferor in ordinary course of business if the bailee has delivered the goods to the buyer or received notification of his rights; or

(c) as against the bailee by good faith dealings of the bailee with the transferor.

(3) A diversion or other change of shipping instructions by the

consignor in a non-negotiable bill of lading which causes the bailee not to deliver to the consignee defeats the consignee's title to the goods if they have been delivered to a buyer in ordinary course of business and in any event defeats the consignee's rights against the bailee.

(4) Delivery pursuant to a non-negotiable document may be stopped by a seller under Section 2-705, and subject to the requirement of due notification there provided. A bailee honoring the seller's instructions is entitled to be indemnified by the seller against any resulting loss or expense

§ 7-505. Indorser not a guarantor for other parties.

The indorsement of a document of title issued by a bailee does not make the indorser liable for any default by the bailee or by previous indorsers. (5A Del. C. 1953, § 7-505; 55 Del. Laws, c. 349.)

RULE §7-505. Indorser not a guarantor for other parties.

The indorsement of a document of title issued by a bailee does not make the indorser liable for any default by the bailee or by previous indorsers.

§ 7-506. Delivery without indorsement: right to compel indorsement.

The transferee of a negotiable document of title has a specifically enforceable right to have his transferor supply any necessary indorsement but the transfer becomes a negotiation only as of the time the indorsement is supplied. (5A Del. C. 1953, § 7-506; 55 Del. Laws, c. 349.)

RULE §7-506. Delivery without indorsement: right to compel indorsement.

The transferee of a negotiable document of title has a specifically enforceable right to have his transferor supply any necessary indorsement but the transfer becomes a negotiation only as of the time the indorsement is supplied.

§ 7-507. Warranties on negotiation or transfer of receipt or bill.

Where a person negotiates or transfers a document of title for value otherwise than as a mere intermediary under the next following section, then unless otherwise agreed he warrants to his immediate purchaser only in addition to any warranty made in selling the goods

(a) that the document is genuine; and

(b) that he has no knowledge of any fact which would impair its validity or worth; and

(c) that his negotiation or transfer is rightful and fully effective with respect to the title to the document and the goods it represents. (5A Del. C. 1953, § 7-507; 55 Del. Laws, c. 349.)

RULE § 7-507. Warranties on negotiation or transfer of receipt or bill.

Where a person negotiates or transfers a document of title for value otherwise than as a mere intermediary under the next following section, then unless otherwise agreed he warrants to his immediate purchaser only in addition to any warranty made in selling the goods

(a) that the document is genuine; and
(b) that he has no knowledge of any fact which would impair its validity or worth; and
(c) that his negotiation or transfer is rightful and fully effective with respect to the title to the document and the goods it represents.

§ 7-508. Warranties of collecting bank as to documents.

A collecting bank or other intermediary known to be entrusted with documents on behalf of another or with collection of a draft or other claim against delivery of documents warrants by such delivery of the documents only its own good faith and authority. This rule applies even though the intermediary has purchased or made advances against the claim or draft to be collected. (5A Del. C. 1953, § 7-508; 55 Del. Laws, c. 349.)

RULE §7-508. Warranties of collecting bank as to documents.

A collecting bank or other intermediary known to be entrusted with documents on behalf of another or with collection of a draft or other claim against delivery of documents warrants by such delivery of the documents only its own good faith and authority. This rule applies even though the intermediary has purchased or made advances against the claim or draft to be collected.

§ 7-509. Receipt or bill: when adequate compliance with commercial contract.

The question whether a document is adequate to fulfill the obligations of a contract for sale or the conditions of a credit is governed by the Articles on Sales (Article 2) and on Letters of Credit (Article 5). (5A Del. C. 1953, § 7-509; 55 Del. Laws, c. 349.)

RULE §7-509. Receipt or bill: when adequate compliance with commercial contract.

The question whether a document is adequate to fulfill the obligations of a contract for sale or the conditions of a credit is governed by the Articles on Sales (Article 2) and on Letters of Credit

CONTRACTS & SALES

LEGAL TRAIL SERIES